The Private Lives of the Pharaohs

The Private Lives
of the Pharaohs

Joyce Tyldesley

NEW YORK

Library of Congress Cataloging-in-Publication Data
Tyldesley, Joyce A.
    The private lives of the pharaohs : unlocking the secrets of Egyptian royalty / Joyce Tyldesley.
    p. cm.
    ISBN 1-57500-154-3
    1. Egypt—Antiquities. 2. Pharaohs. 3. Egypt—History—To 332 B.C. I. Title.
DT61.T85 2001
932'.01'0922—dc21
00-054490

The publisher has made every effort to secure permission to reproduce copyrighted material and
would like to apologize should there have been any errors or omissions.

A TV6 production for Thirteen/WNET New York in association with Channel 4.
A companion to the *Secrets of the Pharaohs* series seen on public television.
Executive in Charge: William R. Grant
Executive Producer: Beth Hoppe
Coordinating Producer: Jared Lipworth

TV Books, L.L.C.
1619 Broadway
New York, NY 10019
www.tvbooks.com

Interior design by Rachel Reiss
Manufactured in the United States of America

Contents

Acknowledgements

FIRSTLY I WOULD LIKE TO THANK RICHARD REISZ AND DEV VARMA FOR PRO-
ducing a television series of outstanding interest and beauty. Tamara Bo-
denham, Lesley Cherry, and Jane Blackmore also deserve my thanks. I
would like to thank Peter Kaufman, Jackie Cohen, Grace Zimmer, and
Rachel Reiss of TV Books for guiding me through the production of this
book. I will always be grateful to Katy Carrington. Finally I would like to
thank all those experts, too numerous to mention individually, whose ded-
ication to Egyptology made the original television series possible.

Introduction

THE DRAMATIC TALE OF THE FOUNDING OF EGYPT IS ENSHRINED IN DYNASTIC legend. Five thousand years ago, or so we are told, the warrior Menes mustered a mighty army and marched northwards along the Nile, subduing and consolidating the independent city-states that threatened to impede his progress. Eventually Menes reached the apex of the Nile Delta, and here he was crowned king of the newly unified land. Upper and Lower Egypt were now one. From this time onwards dynastic civilization flourished, remaining remarkably constant in its self-imposed cultural isolation as the world outside the Nile Valley gradually shifted and changed.

The civilization that had started with such an impressive bang was, however, destined to go out with a faint whimper. In 332 BCE Alexander the Great arrived to conquer a weary Egypt already weakened by years of political in-fighting and a brief period of Persian rule. Now Egypt was quickly assimilated into the Graeco-Roman world, her unique culture first debased and then irretrievably lost. Time marched mercilessly on and, as the Christian era was ended by the Arab conquest in the seventh century CE, as the desert sands smothered her temples and tombs, Egypt's past splendours were entirely forgotten until only the Bible and a handful of classical texts preserved the memory of a once glorious nation.

Buried beneath her sands, three thousand years of dynastic Egypt have left a remarkable legacy. A fortunate combination of evidence—human remains, monumental buildings, rock-cut tombs, writings and much, much more—preserved by a unique combination of climatic and geographical conditions, offers the modern observer the chance to reconstruct the lost lives of those who once lived and died along the Nile. The limiting factor in our understanding of this past society is, and always has been, our ability to recover and interpret the preserved data.

Egyptology is a relatively new discipline that has been forced to evolve at a startling pace. Two hundred years ago Egypt's earliest archaeologists were little more than officially sanctioned treasure hunters. Unable to read the hieroglyphs that decorated temple and tomb, unaware of even the most rudimentary principles of scientific excavation and uninterested in the collection of the mundane and the study of the ordinary, their concern was with the exposure and, if possible, the collection of the more obvious and impressive remains. They sought and seized the monumental pieces that spoke of kings and death, and it seemed to many that knowledge of ancient Egypt could expand no further.

In 1822 Jean François Champollion announced his decipherment of hieroglyphics. Egyptologists were liberated by their hard-won understanding of the long-lost language. They were now able to read the words of their long-dead subjects and, while the written record was undeniably incomplete, much of the previously inexplicable was suddenly made gloriously clear. For the first time it became possible to reconstruct Egypt's long and complicated history and to attempt an understanding of the convoluted theology which had obviously underpinned so many aspects of dynastic life. The Egyptians were revealed, not as a gloomy people obsessed by dying, but as a vibrant, happy nation who loved life so much that they planned to live beyond death. This ability to read the ancient texts was to have a great impact on the development of Egyptology, which now very much became a text-based discipline. Archaeology—grubbing around in sand and dirt, searching for elusive clues—was seen by many as an inferior, even unnecessary option. Unfortunately, as many of the texts were concerned with Egypt's royalty and upper classes, and with matters of death, this concentration on the written evidence biased the historical record, causing the ordinary, illiterate members of society to drop even further out of sight.

Nevertheless, as the linguists set to work in their dark libraries, translating their texts and indulging in scholarly arguments over obscure signs and phrases, out in the sun the excavators too were rethinking their approach. Developments in the theory of Egyptological excavation and conservation were slowly but steadily influenced by developments in the archaeology of less well-preserved societies, so that as the nineteenth century progressed treasure hunting digs were gradually transformed into controlled scientific environments. Now the emphasis was on the recording and storing of all data, no matter how apparently trivial. The potsherds, textiles and bones that had once been discarded in the frenzied hunt for colossal statuary were now gathered up and stored, and the new-style excavators even started to excavate the waste-dumps of their predecessors in an attempt to rescue the small-scale evidence of the past. Mummies, once regarded as rather tasteless, essentially uninformative curiosities valued only for the jewellery hidden beneath their bandages, now took their rightful place among the important archaeological finds, as recognition grew that mummies should be treated with the respect due to a dead human being, no matter how old.

With the twentieth century came another very important change. The rapid scientific progress that has seen man on the moon and the mapping of human DNA has allowed modern Egyptologists to expand their repertoire of analytical approaches. Computing, chemistry, biology, botany, geology and medicine all have an important contribution to make towards our understanding of the past. These techniques, part of a multi-disciplinary approach that also includes the more traditional methodologies, are now being used to tackle questions which would have been unanswerable only twenty years ago. In particular, the field of mummy studies has changed beyond recognition as the bodies that were once unwrapped and destroyed as a form of public entertainment are now subjected to the most detailed of medical scrutiny. Today's Egyptologist is as likely to be found bent over a microscope in a lab as shovelling sand on an Indiana Jones-style dig, and DNA analysis now ranks alongside hieroglyph analysis as a standard research tool. The results of this new integrated approach can be spectacular.

THIS BOOK HAS EVOLVED FROM THE CHANNEL 4 TELEVISION SERIES *THE Private Lives of the Pharaohs,* a series that demonstrates just how far the Egyptologist–scientist has gone along the road to understanding the past. We will be examining three dynastic case studies taken from three different eras, each involving a combination of scientific and traditional techniques and each attempting to tackle one or more specific problems. Each case study uses the bodies of the Egyptians themselves as a means of exploring their history.

Case Study One goes back some forty-five centuries to address some of the oldest and most frequently asked questions in Egyptology—who exactly built the Great Pyramid of Giza, how did they do it, and why? Case Study Two, set in the claustrophobic 18th Dynasty royal court, examines the relationships between the members of the Tuthmoside royal family and seeks to determine what exactly brought about the collapse of the Amarna Age. Finally, Case Study Three takes as its starting point the mummified body of a temple singer, Asru, and draws from this remarkable conclusions concerning aspects of life at the very end of the New Kingdom.

Egyptology, with its specialized jargon, its dynasties and its inordinately lengthy string of curiously named pharaohs, can be daunting for the uninitiated. Chapter 1, a brief history of the dynastic age, therefore sets the scene for those readers unfamiliar with the story of ancient Egypt.

Note on Spellings

THE ANCIENT EGYPTIANS WROTE THEIR TEXTS WITHOUT VOWELS, USING A VA-riety of consonants some of which are not found in our own alphabet. By convention, in translation, vowels are inserted to make the ancient words legible to the modern reader. However, different authors use different, equally valid spellings for the same name. This occasionally causes confu-sion. Tutankhamen, for example, may also appear as Tutankamun while Ramesses is also Ramses and Ramesse. In this book I have used the most simple and widely accepted version of each name.

Time Line

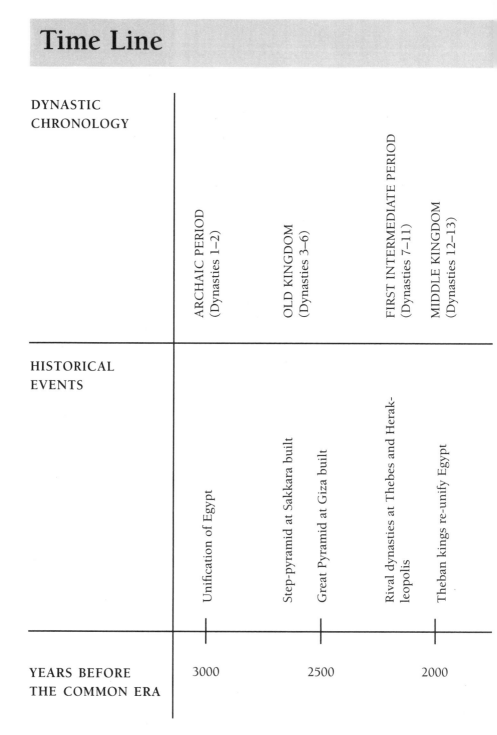

DYNASTIC CHRONOLOGY

ARCHAIC PERIOD (Dynasties 1–2)

OLD KINGDOM (Dynasties 3–6)

FIRST INTERMEDIATE PERIOD (Dynasties 7–11)

MIDDLE KINGDOM (Dynasties 12–13)

HISTORICAL EVENTS

Unification of Egypt

Step-pyramid at Sakkara built

Great Pyramid at Giza built

Rival dynasties at Thebes and Herakleopolis

Theban kings re-unify Egypt

YEARS BEFORE THE COMMON ERA

3000   2500   2000

SECOND INTERMEDIATE PERIOD
(Dynasties 14–17)

NEW KINGDOM
(Dynasties 18–20)

THIRD INTERMEDIATE PERIOD
(Dynasties 21–25)

LATE PERIOD
(Dynasties 26–31)

PTOLEMAIC PERIOD

Last of the great royal pyramids built

Hyksos kings in the North
Theban kings in the South

Amarna Period
Tutankhamen
Ramesses II

Kings at Tanis
Nubian kings
Assyrian invasion

Egypt conquered by Persians
Alexander the Great expels Persians

Egypt part of the Roman Empire

1500   1000   500   CE 0

Part One

▲ ▲ ▲ ▲ ▲ ▲ ▲

The Gift
of the
Nile

CHAPTER ONE

Birth and Death
of a Civilization

THE RIVER NILE, LOADED WITH THE WATERS OF LAKE TANA, FLOWS NORTH-
wards on a journey of some forty-eight hundred kilometres (three thousand miles) before branching to form the Nile Delta and emptying into the
Mediterranean Sea. Over a thousand kilometres (seven hundred miles)
from journey's end it passes through a series of cataracts and enters the ancient kingdom of Egypt, bringing much needed water to an otherwise arid
landscape and depositing a rich soil along its banks. Here, throughout the
three thousand years of the dynastic age (c. 3100–332 BCE), the Nile acted
not only as the national reservoir but also as the main drain and principal
highway, uniting the towns and cities of this long, thin land.

The fortunate combination of north-flowing river and breezes blowing
southwards made river transport an easy and practical affair and there was
no need for the ancient Egyptians to invest in a nationwide network of
roads. Meanwhile the fertile river silt that allowed the development of agri-
culture also offered a plentiful and easily accessible building material: for
thousands of years Egypt's domestic architects used sun-dried mud-bricks,
reserving the expensive and unwieldy stone for their temples and tombs.

When the classical historian Herodotus visited Egypt at the very end of the dynastic age he well understood what he saw. "Egypt," he wrote in an often-quoted phrase, "is the gift of the Nile."

Civilization had developed slowly but surely along the Nile Valley. The river, the only reliable source of water for hundreds of miles, had attracted the earliest hunter–fisher–gatherers and their prey, and archaeologists have found traces of occupation in the form of stone tools dating to several hundred thousand years ago. Eventually, during the sixth millennium BCE, the first settled agriculturists arrived. Taking full advantage of the thin strip of fertile soil trapped between the river and the desert sands, the new farmers supplemented their hunting and fishing diets with crops of wheat and barley, manufacturing clay pots and woven baskets in which to store their surplus. First villages, then towns and finally cities developed, their residents dwelling in well-made houses of basketwork and mud-brick linked together by unplanned, winding streets.

Each town or village worshipped its own deity: a god or goddess who provided a convincing explanation for the otherwise inexplicable traumas of daily life. By now the dead were usually, but not always, buried in designated cemeteries away from the living area. Here, as the tradition of providing grave goods developed, archaeologists have encountered the evidence of a more material age: the dead were now wrapped in woven mats or skins, furnished with jewellery and ornaments, needles and combs. It seems that these early Egyptians already felt the need to enter the next life fully equipped with the spoils of this one.

Technically, Egypt's history starts at the point of unification in c.3100 BCE, the time when the chain of city-states and their satellite agricultural communities united to form one long, unwieldy country stretching from the Delta in the north to Aswan in the south. This new land was ruled by one all-powerful king or pharaoh. The story of the valiant Menes marching northwards to claim his crown is, unfortunately, unlikely to be true. Unification was almost certainly a lengthy and complex affair, with the independent communities gradually realizing the advantages of bonding together until two distinct power-bases emerged: the north, or Lower Egypt including the Delta region, and the south, or Upper Egypt. This north–south divide was to feature heavily in subsequent dynastic history.

Irrigation, often cited as a unifying force, was perhaps less significant than we might suppose. Efficient land and water management would always be matters of some importance, with the digging of communal canals and dykes classed as state projects. But Egypt, with her abundant natural resources, did not experience the population pressures that caused other emerging states to regulate their water supply from the very beginning.

The unique annual inundation made large-scale, nationwide artificial irrigation unnecessary. Every year, summer rains in faraway Ethiopia swelled the White and Blue Niles, tributaries of the Nile. In Egypt this added burden of water caused the river to burst its banks and flood its valley. The cemeteries, safe in the desert sands, and the mud-brick houses, prudently built on raised ground, remained dry. Meanwhile the low-lying fields lay lost underwater while their farmers, unable to perform their agricultural duties, became free to undertake other work.

Eventually the waters retreated, leaving behind a highly fertile, mineral- and water-rich soil, a series of filled lakes to provide further water and an added bonus of thousands of stranded fish that could be collected, dried and salted to provide against leaner times. The farmers set to work, sowing their seeds by hand in October/November and harvesting a generous crop in March. The empty fields were then left to bake in the hot, sterilizing sun, a fallow period that ensured the eradication of pests and diseases. If all went well, only the most outlying of fields plus the luxuriant gardens surrounding the villas of the upper classes would need extra irrigation in the form of the shadoof, a levered bucket used to raise water from the canal to the land. However, should the Nile fail to function as expected—if the floods were either too high or too low—there could be problems. Nile levels were subjected to regular monitoring at specially constructed "Nilometers" and prudent pharaohs stored surpluses in massive warehouses to provide against famine. Today, following the building of the Aswan High Dam, the Nile floods her valley no more.

Egypt's unusual geography focused attention inwards, towards her dominant river and its narrow lining of fertile soil. Beyond the "Blackland" lay the "Redland": mile upon mile of hot, dry, inhospitable desert where only the dead and the occasional nomad could find a home. Beyond this again were the cliffs that protected Egypt from unwelcome visitors. The progression from water to soil to sand—from divine to living to dead—was an immediate and obvious symmetry that was to play an important part in the development of theology and funerary tradition.

Egypt was not only a fertile country, she was rich in stone, precious metals, mud and papyrus; a shortage of wood was the only potential problem for those wishing to build a mighty nation. There was therefore little need for most Egyptians to venture beyond the well-regulated safety of their valley. Inevitably, to the isolated, protected valley dwellers, the unknown and uncontrolled world beyond Egypt appeared a frightening place. Even in the less confined Delta region, with its Mediterranean coast and Near Eastern land bridge, there was still a tendency to look inwards rather than abroad. It is important not to overstate this geographical and cultural isolation; trade with the Near East was important from the very beginning of Egypt's history. And yet, throughout the dynastic era, foreigners—those who did not obey pharaoh's rule—were considered inferior, their non-Egyptian habits the object of deep suspicion. This attitude contributed greatly to the conservative nature of Egyptian art and crafts, which today allows even the most ill-informed observer to recognize an Egyptian tomb painting at a glance.

The Nile contributed not only to the development of Egyptian civilization, but also to the idiosyncratic preservation of her remains which, as even the most casual museum visitor will have noticed, are heavily biased towards religion and death. Homes and fields had to be built close to the life-giving river, with domestic architecture sited wherever possible on the levees and natural raised areas that would protect them from the annual flooding. Today, almost without exception, these domestic sites are lost beneath more recent farms and towns, with much of their mud-brick dissolved in the Nile damp so that only their stone architecture—their statuary and temples—remains.

Once-mighty Thebes, capital of the south, has largely disappeared beneath present-day Luxor and is now largely represented by the Karnak and Luxor temples. Memphis, the equivalent northern capital, is today a series of modern villages built on low, ancient mounds with only the ruined temple of Ptah and a fallen colossus of Ramesses II to hint at lost grandeur. Ramesses' own Delta capital, the glorious Pi-Ramesse, which once included a magnificent palace, four or more temples, an army barracks and a thriving port, has vanished so completely that after decades of argument archaeologists have only just agreed on its location. In stark contrast, much of the architecture of the dead lies preserved in the desert sands, whose arid sterility protects both artefacts and human tissue against damp, decay and modern development.

WHATEVER THE PROCESS, IT SEEMS THAT AT LEAST SOME BLOOD WAS SHED IN the struggle to impose a single monarch on the newly created Egyptian throne. The first documented king of the unified land is Narmer, a southern warrior and perhaps the inspiration for the legendary Menes. A ceremonial stone palette now housed in Cairo Museum shows Narmer at the very moment of his triumph. Followed by his sandal-bearer, and wearing the distinctive white crown of Upper Egypt, Narmer pauses in the act of ritual murder. A club is raised in his right hand while with his left he grasps the hair of the ignoble enemy who cringes at his feet. The enemy, representative of all Egypt's foes, understands that he can expect no mercy; already pharaoh is ruthless in eliminating the enemies of Egypt. The reverse of the palette shows a slightly more peaceful scene. Narmer, now sporting the red crown of Lower Egypt and once again accompanied by his loyal sandal-bearer, marches with a troop of soldiers whose ornate standards may well represent the symbols of the newly unified provinces. In front of this procession lie the decapitated victims of war, their heads stored neatly between their knees.

With unification we encounter the first Egyptian writings, and from this point onwards we are able to follow the ancient Egyptian practice of using individual reigns to date historical events. Thus, to take an example, the famous Bronze Age Battle of Kadesh is dated by both ancient Egyptians and modern Egyptologists to Year 5 of the reign of Ramesses II, and everyone understands what is meant by this date. When an attempt is made to translate Year 5 of the reign of Ramesses II into modern calendar dates there is immediate scholastic argument; did Ramesses live from 1279 to 1213 BCE, or from 1290 to 1224?

Preserved within the temples and tombs of Karnak, Sakkara and Abydos we find lists of Egyptian kings stretching back from the New Kingdom

to the Early Dynastic age. Historians have been able to project this list for-
wards so that today we have a register of Egyptian monarchs, covering
some three thousand years, which we know to be broadly correct. By convention this list is divided into groups, or dynasties, of related monarchs.
These dynasties start with Dynasty 1, the point of unification, and end
with Dynasty 31 and the arrival of Alexander the Great. The Dynasties are
then further agglomerated into Kingdoms (times of strong government),
Intermediate Periods (times of weak government), and the confused and
somewhat ignominious Late Period that sees the end of the dynastic age.

What is termed the Archaic Period of unification was followed by the Old
Kingdom, a time of strict feudal rule. The king was now accepted as the
sole owner of both the land and its people, an ownership that gave him the
right to requisition labour as and when he pleased. As an acknowledged
semi-divine being, the king had also become the sole link between mortals
and the state pantheon, the collection of nationally dominant deities that
had evolved from the more localized cults of predynastic times. Pharaoh
was now the chief priest of every god and, although he was able to employ
deputy priests to assist him in his duties, technically it was he alone who
could make the divine offerings necessary to please the gods. He stood as
his people's representative before the gods, and the gods' representative before the people. After death, his spirit might leave the tomb to dwell as a
star, or to sail in the solar boat of Re. Most important of all: to the king fell
the awesome responsibility of maintaining *maat*, the state of rightness or
status quo which indicated that everything and everyone was functioning
correctly in Egypt. This concept of *maat*, and the perceived need to keep
things in an unchanging state of correctness in order to avoid the dreaded
state of chaos, was to persist throughout the dynastic age, reinforcing the
authority of the pharaoh. Everyone knew that a kingless Egypt would be a
dangerous affront to *maat*; the king was therefore essential to Egypt.

Egypt was now governed from the north, with Memphis serving as the
administrative capital and Sakkara and Giza acting as the royal cemeteries. A select band of courtiers drawn from the interrelated ranks of Egypt's
élite assisted pharaoh in his rule, while in the provinces the local governors, or nomarchs, retained their inherited responsibility for the efficient
running of their territory.

This was the age of the pyramids, including the Giza pyramids which form the basis of Case Study One, when the devotees of the northern sun-god Re attempted to build royal tombs that would serve as a physical bridge between the earth and the sky. Tombs, and tomb security, had become matters of some importance. Theology now decreed that the physical survival of the dead body was essential for the survival of the soul beyond death, and already the undertakers were experimenting with mummification as a means of preserving the corpse. The earliest mummies were prone to decay and few have survived to bear witness to this developing art. Fortunately, some of the more robust later dynastic mummies have managed to avoid the attentions of those who would strip them for their jewels, unroll them as public entertainment, burn them as fuel, grind them up as medicine and even pulp them for use in the manufacture of paint or brown paper. These mummies are now recognized as forming a priceless human data bank, storing the details of ancient lives.

While a dead king might leave the confines of the grave, his subjects were condemned to pass all eternity isolated within their tombs. Not unreasonably, those who could afford it sought to make their confinement bearable by providing all the luxuries, including space, they felt they would need. Grave goods were considered essential; these would be used by the spirit after death. Unfortunately everyone knew that the burials of the nobles contained untold treasures, and tomb robbery quickly developed into a fine art. Only the graves of the poor, those buried with little pomp and fewer goods, survived the attentions of the thieves.

We do not know what caused the highly centralized Old Kingdom bureaucracy to fail, although a series of low Nile levels leading to poor harvests and food shortages can have done little to help the struggling monarch impose his waning authority over a dissatisfied land. The First Intermediate Period saw the provinces once again self-reliant, and the hereditary nomarchs assuming increased power as the collapse of central government left no one in overall control. It was almost as if the pre-unification jostlings for supremacy were starting all over again as the now independent city-states grouped themselves into advantageous political alliances. Eventually there were two main centres of power and two rival courts: a Theban dynasty ruling in the south and a Herakleopolitan dynasty controlling the north.

Once again it was the southern dynasty which was to triumph. The Theban kings were able to reimpose central authority, moving north to establish a new capital city at Itj-Tawy, close to the old capital of Memphis, and founding a pyramid necropolis at nearby Lisht. The new pharaohs, astute politicians, gradually took measures to reduce the influence of the nomarchs whose provincial powers posed a permanent threat to the authority of the monarch. Under Senwosret III a reorganization of local government ensured that from now on Egypt would be run by a professional civil service drawn from the ranks of the educated middle and upper classes, with pharaoh retaining ultimate power.

The Middle Kingdom recovered from the assassination of its founder, Amenemhat I, to experience a period of internal stability and external adventure. Literature and the arts flourished, there was increased foreign trade and a series of successful military campaigns that laid down the foundations of the Egyptian empire in Nubia. Now the royal sculptors subtly altered their approach and the official image of the king—to modern eyes at least—changes from the imperious autocratic demi-god of the Old Kingdom to that of a more human, careworn king burdened with the responsibility of caring for his people.

The Nile Delta was prosperous and stable, an attractive prospect to the Semitic peoples whose own less fertile homelands were now being threatened by immigrants from further east. Throughout the Middle Kingdom "Asiatics" had been arriving in ever increasing numbers to settle peacefully in the north. Initially absorbed into the local towns and villages, these groups now started to form their own semi-independent communities. At the same time the provincial governors started to rebel against their loss of inherited authority. This political instability, combined with a series of abnormally high Nile floods plus internal squabbling within the royal family, signalled the beginning of the end. The Middle Kingdom collapsed with Egypt once again fragmented, and the Second Intermediate Period dawned with the Nubian kingdom of Kerma ruling in the extreme south, an Egyptian dynasty ruling from Thebes and the Hyksos, Palestinian invaders, ruling in the north from the new capital of Avaris.

The Hyksos were to control northern Egypt for over a century, adopting the traditional titles of native-born Egyptian kings. They proved to be good monarchs. Under their stewardship the Delta flourished, foreign relations improved and a series of exotic imports, including new pottery and bronze-working techniques, stimulated the insular native Egyptian craftsmen. The semi-professional Egyptian army benefited enormously from the new regime: the design of armour, dagger and sword each underwent swift improvement, while the introduction of the harnessed horse, the two-wheeled horse-drawn chariot and the highly effective compound bow transformed the somewhat ramshackle military into an efficient fighting machine. Nevertheless, the ignominy of foreign kings on pharaoh's throne was hard for the intensely patriotic Egyptians to bear, and the essentially peaceful Hyksos rule was to go down in official Egyptian history as a terrible time of lawlessness and bloodshed.

The local Theban dynasty were reluctant to accept their reduced role. Initially on good diplomatic terms with their Hyksos neighbours, the relationship slowly deteriorated until outright war was declared. After a series of fierce battles which saw the death of his father and older brother, King Ahmose succeeded in expelling the Hyksos and regaining control of the north. He then turned his attention southwards, crushing the Nubian rebels and reimposing Egyptian rule. Ahmose, founder of the New Kingdom and first king of the 18th Dynasty, was followed by a succession of successful warrior kings so that Egypt, once remarkable for her insularity and her intolerance of anything non-Egyptian, rapidly acquired an empire stretching from Nubia to Syria plus a sphere of influence reaching far beyond this. Tribute and taxes poured inwards and, as the royal coffers filled to overflowing, financed the ambitious civil projects that now saw many of Egypt's mud-brick temples converted into magnificent stone monuments.

This increased wealth filtered downwards and the middle classes, much in demand as scribes and accountants, prospered. Artisans, too, benefited from the boom-inspired demand for material goods and it was only the peasants and serfs, those who dwelt at the very base of the social pyramid, whose lives remained fundamentally unchanged.

The boom was to have an obvious effect on the industry of death, with the newly rich middle classes clamouring to enjoy the same funerary privileges as their social superiors. Mummification became accessible to all who could afford it, and sales of funerary papyri, coffins and jewellery rocketed. By now the Afterlife, once the exclusive home of dead kings, had become democratized. Everyone, given the survival of the body, could now aspire to leave the tomb and dwell for ever alongside Osiris in his beautiful, peaceful Field of Reeds.

The new kings remained loyal to their southern traditions. The Theban god Amen, "The Hidden One," was credited with the victory against the Hyksos, forcing the northern Re to take a back seat as Thebes emerged as Egypt's religious capital. Here, on the east bank of the Nile, the Karnak temple, home to Amen and his family, underwent a centuries-long programme of refurbishment and expansion as successive monarchs vied to express their piety in stone. Meanwhile, on the west bank in a remote, hidden valley, workmen started to excavate the new-style rock-cut tombs of the pharaohs. Here it was hoped that the kings would rest in peace for all eternity, their precious mummies protected from the robbers who preyed remorselessly on Egypt's cemeteries. The tradition of burying expensive artefacts alongside the dead was proving to be a costly one.

One New Kingdom pharaoh was not happy to accept the supremacy of Amen and the increasing influence of his priests. As Akhenaten took his throne in *c.* 1353 BCE, Egypt had never been more powerful or more wealthy. Her court sparkled as the sophisticated centre of the cosmopolitan eastern Mediterranean world and her king was the envy of his brother monarchs. Akhenaten, however, was not prepared to play the part of a conventional Egyptian monarch and his reign saw a swift reversal of Egypt's fortunes. Totally absorbed in his own religious experiment, Akhenaten defied *maat* and turned his back on the state gods. Thebes and Memphis were abandoned as a new capital, Akhetaten or Amarna, sprang up in Middle Egypt. Here Akhenaten worshipped a single deity, the Sun's disk or Aten. Isolated at Amarna, Akhenaten showed little interest in events outside his own narrow sphere. After seventeen years of heretic rule he died, leaving Egypt weak and vulnerable, with much of her empire lost and her internal economy corrupted.

Akhenaten was followed by a series of short-lived kings including Tutankhamen, one of the subjects of our Case Study Two, and the 18th Dynasty slowly faltered to a halt. In the absence of an obvious heir the throne passed first to a highly competent general, Horemheb, and then to a family of northerners from the Delta region. The Ramesside kings, modelling themselves on Egypt's mighty warrior pharaohs, were able to reverse their country's decline and ushered in the final stage of the New Kingdom. By the time Ramesses II came to the throne the traditional gods were once more secluded in their rightful temples and Egypt's empire was substantially restored. It was obvious to all that *maat* had returned. There was, however, one important difference. As northerners, the 19th Dynasty kings felt no personal allegiance to Amen and, although Thebes retained her role as the royal necropolis, the Ramesside era saw increased political and religious activity in the north. Here, in the eastern Delta close to the old Hyksos capital of Avaris, a new capital city, Pi-Ramesse, was built and here, after almost seventy years on the throne, the aged Ramesses II died.

Ramesses had been a prolific father: the immediate succession was clear, but the plethora of royal descendants was soon to cause problems as those closest to the throne started to jockey for position. At the same time, external pressures were beginning to threaten Egypt's peace. The late New Kingdom was a time of extensive population shift in the eastern Mediterranean and Egypt, fertile and stable, was a prime target for displaced nomadic groups. Fifty years after the death of Ramesses II, Ramesses III was able to repel the sea-borne invaders who menaced the Delta, but his military victories proved expensive and the royal coffers, no longer filled by tribute from the east, were worryingly empty. Inflation, civil disobedience and an increasingly powerful priesthood of Amen followed and, as eight further Ramesses succeeded to the throne, the economic crisis slowly but surely worsened with low Nile levels now adding to Egypt's problems.

Gradually pharaoh became impotent, his bureaucracy irredeemably corrupt. First the eastern empire, then Nubia, were lost and, although the much-looted Theban necropolis was still in use, the south was now effectively controlled by the High Priest of Amen. The end of the New Kingdom, the age of Asru, subject of Case Study Three, saw Egypt once again divided, with a local dynasty ruling the north from Tanis and the High Priests of Amen assuming royal titles to rule the south from Thebes.

The Third Intermediate Period dawned with surprisingly cordial relations between the Tanite kings and the Theban priests. Royal marriages were a practical means of cementing diplomatic alliances, and a succession of princesses now sailed southwards. Initially sent to wed the reigning High Priest, these princesses were later to become the "God's Wife of Amen," an ancient title that had been revived to allow the daughter of the Tanite king to become the most powerful and wealthy priestly figure in Egypt. Perhaps inevitably, the good relationship between south and north eventually collapsed and the Tanite kings found themselves under pressure in the Delta. A confusing period followed, with various local chieftains, many of Libyan descent, simultaneously proclaiming themselves pharaoh.

Nubia, for so long Egypt's southern province, was by now fully independent with her own ruling dynasty. Kashta, king of Nubia, determined to take full advantage of Egypt's weakened state and, in 770 BCE, marched northward as far as Thebes. Here he had his sister proclaimed God's Wife of Amen, a political ritual that effectively confirmed his own right to rule Egypt. Kashta was proclaimed King of Upper and Lower Egypt, but it was his successor, Piye, who reached the Nile Delta and so reunited the divided land. A century of stability followed, with the new dynasty taking full credit for the restoration of *maat*. Like the Hyksos before them, the Nubian pharaohs adopted all the trappings of Egyptian kingship and respected the Egyptian gods, although they shunned the royal burial grounds and returned home to be buried under Egyptian-looking pyramids which, when first discovered, caused intense confusion among Egyptologists.

Egypt was now at peace, but outside her borders the international situation was deteriorating rapidly. Egypt could no longer cut herself off from external events. In 671 BCE an Assyrian invasion force managed to capture the Nile Delta, forcing King Tanutamen to flee southwards, to Nubia. Nubia was to remain under the control of his dynasty for a further 350 years. Meanwhile, Egyptian resistance sparked a further Assyrian assault, and in 663 the Assyrians penetrated as far south as Thebes. Once-proud Egypt was reduced to the ignoble status of a province, her Delta now ruled by the Assyrian-appointed Saite puppet kings.

The beginning of the Late Period saw the Assyrians removed and the country once more reunited under the now autonomous Saite dynasty. This was to be the last flourishing of Egyptian independence, a prosperous time of determined Egyptian revival when the Saites sought to recapture the glories of the Old Kingdom by replicating the artistic and architectural achievements of earlier kings. The Saite kings revered the builders of the three Giza pyramids, and burial close to these royal tombs was once again regarded as beneficial. History, however, could not be repeated and the Old Kingdom was now a faraway country indeed. In 525 BCE the Persian army conquered Egypt, installing their own dynasties which were interspersed by a brief period of local rule. Finally, in 332 BCE, Alexander the Great arrived in Egypt. The dynastic age was well and truly ended.

Part Two

▲ ▲ ▲ ▲ ▲ ▲

The Lost City of the Pyramid Builders

The Lost City
of the
Pyramid Builders

When King Cheops succeeded to the throne of Egypt he plunged into all manner of wickedness. He closed the temples and banned the people from offering to the gods. Instead he forced them without exception to toil for him. Some were made to drag blocks of stone from the quarries to the Nile. Others received the stone blocks when they had crossed the river by boat, and dragged them to the chosen hill site. A hundred thousand men toiled constantly, being relieved every three months by a new contingent of labourers. It took ten years' oppression of the people to make the causeway which would allow the passage of the blocks . . . to level the top of the hill and to prepare the underground chambers which Cheops planned to use as a burial vault. . . . The pyramid itself took twenty years to build . . . .

Herodotus, *Histories*, Book 2: 124

WHEN THE GREEK WRITER HERODOTUS TOURED EGYPT IN THE FIFTH CEN-
tury BCE, the Great Pyramid of the 4th Dynasty King Cheops, who is today
better known by his Egyptian name Khufu, was already over two thousand
years old. Like any other diligent tourist, Herodotus visited the Giza
plateau where he marvelled at its three pyramids—including the Great
Pyramid—and listened to the tales told by the local guides. By including
these stories in his *Histories* he offered the world the first explanation of
how and by whom the pyramids were built. To Herodotus, a Greek accustomed to the idea of state-owned slaves, the use of forced labourers on
royal projects made perfect sense.

Five hundred years later his explanation was to be picked up and elab-
orated by the Jewish historian Josephus. Making a mistake of over a
thousand years in his chronology, Josephus believed that he knew who
these unfortunate slaves had been: "The Egyptians compelled them [the
Hebrews] to cut many channels for their river, and to build walls and
ramparts for their cities which would hold back the flooding river. . . .
They also forced them to work on the pyramids, and by this work,
ground them down."

Two thousand years after Herodotus' visit, the pyramids have retained
their power to fascinate. Tourists still flock to the Giza plateau where they
too marvel and listen to the ancient tales told by the modern guides. Most
of these visitors believe firmly that they understand how the pyramids were
built. Herodotus' tale of slavery—of thousands upon thousands of slaves
labouring to fulfil pharaoh's dream—has become widely accepted, due in
no small part to the work of Hollywood directors who have included such
scenes in their epic works. Few who have seen celluloid slaves—often of
Semitic appearance—toiling, falling and dying in front of the Great Pyramid will doubt that this can be anything other than a faithful reconstruction of past events.

Given that the Old Kingdom pharaohs lacked the sophisticated tools and
machinery necessary for our own building projects, it seems valid at first
sight to assume that they must have relied on large-scale forced manpower
for the erection of the world's largest monument. But is there any evidence
to support this theory? The Egyptians themselves have left no written account of the building of their pyramids and so we are forced to turn to ar-

chaeology in our quest for the truth. Archaeology has obliged with a series of spectacular finds that have prompted Egyptologists to reconsider the three essential questions of the pyramid age: who, how and why? Work still in progress in the shadow of the Giza pyramids has now started to reveal the hitherto hidden lives of the pyramid workforce. By learning more about the people who actually built the pyramids, by moving from the realm of theory to knowledge, from kings to commoners, we are offered the opportunity of gaining an insight into dynastic society as a whole.

In the words of Egyptologist and pyramid expert Mark Lehner: "What we have been doing so far is opening small windows on to this ancient reality. It is this information that brings the people back to life, that allows us to reconstruct their lives."

CHAPTER TWO

When?
The History of
the Pyramid Kings

Quite clearly, in order to mobilize a large work-force to build a pyramid such as the Great Pyramid at Giza, the court needed to have absolute control of resources, both manpower and other economic resources. And so what we see at the time of the Giza pyramids really lays the foundation for Egyptian civilization later on.

Egyptologist Toby Wilkinson

AT THE BEGINNING OF THE DYNASTIC AGE THERE WAS NO STONE ARCHITEC-ture in Egypt. In approximately 2630 BCE the chancellor and high priest of Re, Imhotep, designed and built a revolutionary new tomb for his master, the 3rd Dynasty king Djoser. In so doing he ensured that his own name would be celebrated throughout the dynastic age and beyond. Imhotep was to be revered as a doctor, a magician, an astronomer and even as a god. For he was the architect of Egypt's first stone building: Imhotep built the Sakkara step-pyramid.

By the dawn of the 3rd Dynasty Egypt was secure and strengthened in her unity. Pharaoh, assisted by ministers drawn from the restricted and close-knit ranks of Egypt's élite, ruled his kingdom from the fortified city and port of Memphis, his influence already extending southwards beyond Aswan into Nubia. Stability and highly centralized control had brought prosperity; now Near Eastern trade, and the exploitation of the mines and quarries of Nubia and Sinai, brought added wealth into the royal treasury. The individual provinces, effectively ruled by hereditary governors or no-marchs based in the provincial capitals, continued to show a degree of in-dependence, but for the moment the nomarchs were content to submit to pharaoh's rule. Meanwhile, oblivious to these political developments, the vast majority of a population of maybe 1.5–2 million lived in small agri-cultural communities grouped around larger townships. Here they con-tinued in time-honoured fashion to harvest the gifts of the Nile.

The provinces would always retain a loyalty to the gods who dwelt in their local mud-brick and reed temples. Already, however, a state pantheon had started to emerge: a divine super-league of local deities who would serve as the national gods of the unified land and who would reinforce the position of their one semi-divine king–priest. The falcon-headed sun-god Re of Heliopolis quickly assumed dominance among his fellow deities; as the divine navigator who each day piloted the dead king through the sky in his solar boat he was to play an important role in the development of pyramid traditions. The falcon, which soared high in the Egyptian sky, was fast becoming an important symbol of kingship. Of growing importance too was Horus of Hierakonpolis, another falcon-headed deity, who was to become the son of the universal mother-goddess Isis and the dead king of the underworld, Osiris. The legend of Horus and Osiris—of a living son avenging his dead father and taking his rightful place on the throne of Egypt—was reflected in the theory of Egyptian kingship with the living pharaoh being seen as Horus, the dead entombed king as his father, Osiris.

The history of the early Old Kingdom is as yet incompletely understood. Dynasties 1 and 2 are classed as the Archaic Period, a fascinating yet confused time of developing centralization and literacy. With the beginning of the 3rd Dynasty we enter the Old Kingdom, an altogether better documented phase, although one which still poses many unanswered questions. The Old Kingdom comprises Dynasties 3–6: the classic pyramid-building dynasties. Djoser, known to his people as Netjerykhet, is accepted as the second monarch of the 3rd Dynasty, following the shadowy King Nebka. We know little of his successors, Sekhemket, Khaba and Huni. The accession of the next pharaoh, Snefru, marks the beginning of the 4th Dynasty in approximately 2575 BCE.

While Snefru has passed into legend as a kindly, wise king whose principal vice seems to have been his fondness for watching nubile women dressed in see-through beaded net dresses, his son and eventual successor, Khufu, has acquired the opposite reputation. The Westcar Papyrus, a fantastic tale of magic and adventure written many years after Khufu's reign, shows us a cruel Khufu quite willing to decapitate a prisoner in order to test his sorcerer's skills in bringing the dead back to life. Herodotus, for one, believed this bad publicity, and it is this image of Khufu as tyrant that colours Herodotus' account of the building of the Great Pyramid. Khufu was followed by his son, Khaefre, and his grandson Menkaure; these three are the builders of the Giza pyramids that today stand as symbols representative of Egypt herself.

The basic pit graves, in-filled holes topped with a mound of sand or gravel, were to remain in use throughout the dynastic age. For Egypt's élite, however, those who might expect to spend all eternity within their tomb, the pit grave was too simple and too sandy, offering as it did little space for the deceased, no storage facilities and no impressive superstructure. In an attempt to provide decent after-living accommodation the élite started to build what are today called mastaba tombs: low, rectangular mud-brick structures built above one or more subterranean rooms and modelled on their actual homes. The kings of the Archaic Period had been buried in ornate mastaba tombs at Abydos. Now the Old Kingdom royal cemeteries lay on the fringes of the western desert close to the capital city.

By the 3rd Dynasty the typical mastaba burial chamber lay at the base of a vertical shaft cut through the bedrock beneath the cemetery sands. Above, the substantially solid superstructure housed one or two small niches in its exterior walls where offerings could be brought. These niches later developed into multi-roomed chapels where friends and relations could bring gifts of food and drink to sustain the spirit of the deceased. The mastaba was a long-lived tomb type, and Egypt's élite would continue to build their tombs in mud-brick and stone as their kings embarked on new and more ambitious plans.

Djoser was not the first Egyptian to include stone in his tomb—the mastaba tombs of Abydos already incorporated various stone elements—but he was the first to completely abandon mud-brick in favour of stone. Mud-brick was not seen as an inferior building material, and it would continue to be used in the construction of the royal palaces until the end of the dynastic age. But there was now a growing recognition that stone would survive far longer. As tombs were intended to last for ever, while palaces, however grand, were essentially temporary structures, this had to be a good thing. If Djoser's tomb could survive intact beneath its stone superstructure his cult and his body, too, were likely to survive, allowing the king to live for ever beyond death.

This sudden ability to build a large-scale stone monument tells us a great deal about the organizational ability of 3rd Dynasty Egypt. Only an extremely well-coordinated state could mobilize the resources needed to carry out such an ambitious project. Not only would the building of a pyramid demand the services of architects, surveyors, accountants, masons and vast numbers of labourers, there would also be a need for those who could provide essential back-up services. The workforce would need to be fed, clothed, equipped and housed for a considerable length of time. Furthermore, the project would have to be completed in the fastest time possible, as no one knew when the king would die.

Although Egypt is endowed with rich quarries, building in stone was always to prove an expensive and time-consuming option. This explains why, as old temples and tombs fell into disuse and disrepair, later pharaohs were happy to rob the sites of their ancestors, re-employing the precious stone blocks in their own monuments. This pillaging has continued almost up to the present day. As a result, although the core of the step-pyramid itself has survived substantially intact, its precious white outer casing and most of its subsidiary buildings vanished in antiquity. Visitors to Sakkara today wonder before modern reconstructions. Fortunately,

Egypt's monuments are now protected by her Antiquities Service and stealing from the ancient sites is regarded as a serious crime.

Djoser's innovative tomb design meant that Egypt's labourers and architects, accustomed to working with small, light, cheap mud-bricks, were now confronted with the prospect of handling, transporting and lifting blocks of expensive stone. While many of these early stone blocks remained mud-brick sized, some weighed a ton or more. The country's masons, too, faced a challenge; their experience of stone-working was varied and not obviously applicable to pyramid construction. The masons who worked in the graveyards had gained experience of cutting the shafts and chambers beneath the mastaba tombs and of dressing the stone elements used in the Abydos cemeteries. On an altogether different scale flint tools had been used for centuries, and craftsmen were practised in the art of working hard-stone vessels, palettes and mace-heads for domestic and ceremonial use. Djoser's workmen now employed rough-cut local limestone for the pyramid core, fine Tura limestone ferried from across the river for an outer-casing that would shimmer and sparkle in the sunlight, and pink granite, transported from faraway Aswan, to line the underground burial chamber.

Just as the mastaba evolved from the pit grave, so Imhotep's step-pyramid evolved from a mastaba-like base. The ancient removal of the outer casing allows us to see that building works progressed in a series of clearly defined stages. This appears to have been a deliberate strategy whereby at any given time the monument was never too far from completion—an important consideration when building a tomb. Initially Imhotep started out with a square, solid, mastaba-like structure with corners oriented to the points of the compass (or to the flow of the Nile and the rising and setting of the sun), the whole building being cased in Tura limestone. This was later enlarged to form a two-stepped mastaba, again dressed with white limestone. A third extension to the eastern side then transformed the mastaba into a more conventional rectangular shape. With slightly more extension the mastaba next became the bottom step of a four-step-pyramid. Finally the base was extended again and a six-step-pyramid evolved. The finished pyramid was to stand some 60 metres (197 feet) high and hold some 330,400 cubic metres (11.6 million cubic feet) of stone, rubble and fill.

Djoser's granite-lined burial chamber lay underneath his pyramid, at the heart of a subterranean maze of corridors and store-rooms that again reflect the constant revision of the original plan. Today this substructure is further complicated by shafts and tunnels excavated by intrepid tomb robbers. Accessed by a deep, wide shaft, the slightly cramped burial chamber could be entered only via a wide hole in the ceiling. Once the interment had taken place, a massive granite plug weighing over three tons would be dropped into place, effectively sealing the chamber. The access shaft would then be filled with the rubble that was intended to guard against thieves. Djoser reigned for at least nineteen years, but his subterranean structure was never completed, and it seems that the king must have died before the final phase of his tomb was finished.

The step-pyramid was provided with a series of satellite buildings and courtyards, the whole rectangular complex being confined within a massive stone wall decorated with recessed panels and entered via a single gateway. These subsidiary buildings serve as confirmation of the already intricate nature of early Old Kingdom funerary theology. As the complex was designed to serve as a cult centre for the worship of the dead king for all eternity, many of the buildings are connected with the rituals of death. Some, including the mortuary temple where the daily offerings would be made, were obviously functional. Others were not: a series of dummy buildings with rubble cores could not be entered by the living but may well have been viewed as accessible to the dead. There was even a second tomb, the "South Tomb," which was built complete with underground chambers and which could have been designed for the use of the dead king's spirit.

However, as the tomb was intended to function as the home of the deceased, the direct equivalent of the royal palace of the living king, much of the pyramid architecture makes references to the rituals of living kingship rather than of death. In a narrow courtyard, lined with dummy buildings, we find a raised platform where it would appear the king, in celebration of his jubilee or *sed*-festival, might sit on the double thrones of Upper and Lower Egypt. A much larger open space, the South Court, housed a throne platform or altar and a pair of hoop-shaped stone cairns. These cairns would be used to represent territorial markers when the king ran his ritual *sed* race—the race which, in theory at least, proved to the gods and the people that the king was fit to continue with his reign.

Djoser's body vanished long ago, presumably torn apart by the thieves who plundered his tomb. All that remain are a mummified left foot, a segment of right arm and assorted pieces of human chest and spine, recovered from the burial chamber of the step-pyramid but not necessarily belonging to its original occupant. All was not, however, lost; Djoser might still have a chance of experiencing eternal life. In the *serdab*, a small, dark, enclosed kiosk next to the mortuary chapel, sits an almost life-sized stone pharaoh. Dressed in a long robe, wig and striped head-cloth and wearing the false beard of kingship, the dead Djoser peers at the land of the living through two eye-holes. This statue had been designed to serve as a substitute for the king's body, providing a physical host where the king's spirit or soul could dwell as offerings were being made. Those who today peep into the darkness of the *serdab* can still see the stern and enigmatic face of a man who, for over four and a half millennia, has sat in solitary splendour contemplating his own divine destiny. This statue is, however, a replica; the original is now safely housed in Cairo Museum.

Djoser had proved that it was possible to build and substantially complete a huge stone monument. Unfortunately his immediate successors were unable to follow his example. To the west of the step-pyramid lie two unexplored remains, possibly two unfinished pyramid enclosures, while to the south-east is a second step-pyramid, the unfinished monument of the short-lived king Sekhemket which would, had it been completed, have been a taller and more impressive monument than that of Djoser. At Za-wiyet el-Aryan, some seven kilometres (around four miles) to the north of Sakkara, stands the ruined and unfinished pyramid of Khaba, today known as the "Layer Pyramid." Once again, it seems, the untimely death of a king had thwarted the architects. Royal longevity was to prove an important, if unpredictable, factor in successful pyramid building.

Snefru, first king of Dynasty 4, may have ruled Egypt for as long as fifty years. This gave him the time to build and substantially complete three large pyramids, earning him the title of the greatest pyramid-builder of all time. Snefru's three monuments contain more than 3.5 million cubic metres (over 120 million cubic feet) of stone, more than the Great Pyramid itself.

The idea that a king might build more than one tomb is to modern eyes a strange one. After all, the king could be buried in only one place at a time and most pharaohs would have been content with just one substantial pyramid. While we have no proven explanation for this excessive building, it may be that Snefru, experiencing technological problems with his first two pyramids, pressed on to build the third. Thus his building programme might be seen as a variation on Imhotep's staged approach, an approach that ensured there was always a tomb available for an unexpected royal death. (A similar situation was to occur in the Middle Kingdom when Amenemhat III built two pyramids, the second being technologically far more advanced than the first.) Alternatively, Snefru may have wished to provide himself with one or more cenotaphs in addition to his tomb. Whatever its explanation, this prolific construction does serve to prove that by Snefru's reign the art of pyramid building had been well and truly mastered. Modern Egyptologists may struggle to understand how the pyramids were built, but Snefru's workforce were in no doubt.

At the new royal necropolis of Meidum, nearly fifty kilometres (thirty miles) to the south of Memphis, Snefru started to build himself a pyramid that evolved, as construction progressed, from a seven-step-pyramid to a more imposing eight steps. Within the pyramid, rather than beneath it, the corbelled burial chamber was reached via a long, sloping passageway. After about fifteen years the site was abandoned unfinished; then, towards the end of Snefru's reign, the workmen returned to convert the step-pyramid into a true pyramid by filling in the steps with a packing of local stone. Eventually the Meidum pyramid collapsed, and it is now represented by a solid tower-like core surrounded by a substantial mountain of rubble and the ruins of the pyramid complex. We do not know when this catastrophe occurred, or what caused it.

This first true pyramid was surrounded by what was to become the blueprint for subsequent pyramid complexes: a mortuary temple built next to the pyramid was linked via a long causeway to a valley temple, itself connected to the river by a purpose-cut canal. This link with the river facilitated the transportation of building materials and, of course, allowed the funeral cortège to travel in state to the pyramid. Gone were the *sed-*

court and the open South Court that had acted as a reminder of Djoser's earthly rule. From now on, the linear pyramid complex would promote the image of the dead king as a divine being, while the pyramid itself would become closely linked with the cult of the sun.

Snefru's two pyramids built at Dahshur show just how far Egypt's architects and builders had come in little more than fifty years. The first pyramid, the southern one, is today known as the "Bent Pyramid" because it changes angle part-way up. It seems that the royal architects, still experimenting with their craft, were too ambitious in designing a pyramid with base angles of 54 degrees and the pyramid was beset by subsidence problems. By changing the angle to 43 degrees stability was restored but the pyramid was in any case abandoned. Snefru would return to the Bent Pyramid towards the end of his reign, and complete it.

The Northern Pyramid, or "Red Pyramid," was started during the period that the other two pyramids lay abandoned. Designed from the outset as an elegant pyramid with a slope of 43 degrees, the North Pyramid shows signs of hurried completion which may well indicate that it had been chosen as the final resting place of the ailing king Snefru. Mummified body parts recovered from the Red Pyramid include a damaged skull, ribs, part of the left foot and a finger. Anatomists have concluded, on the basis of these remains, that the deceased died when just past middle age; we may therefore assume either that Snefru ascended to the throne as a young man, or that these are not the remnants of Snefru.

Khufu, son of Snefru, survived three older brothers to inherit his father's throne. By tradition he is accorded a reign of twenty-three years although many experts believe, on the basis of his extensive building programme, that he may actually have ruled for far longer; Herodotus suggests that he reigned for fifty years. It is a curious irony that the author of Egypt's greatest monument is today represented by a single seated ivory carving, approximately 7.5 centimetres (3 inches) high, recovered from Abydos where it had apparently served as a votive figurine offered to the god Osiris. It is not clear whether this figurine was carved during Khufu's reign or whether, as seems likely, it is a later work of art. Nor, given the size of the piece, is it possible to read much into the interpretation of the king's features. However, this miniature Khufu, wearing what is almost certainly a broken red crown and seated on a throne, appears a placid, benign pharaoh, far removed from the evil tyrant of Herodotus' tale.

Khufu had the courage—or the folly—to build not several smaller-scale monuments, but one enormous one. Such temerity suggests that he may have been a relatively young man, confident of a long reign, at the time of his succession in approximately 2580 BCE. His chosen necropolis was the Giza plateau which stood close by his capital city, Memphis. Khufu's confidence was to prove fully justified. His Great Pyramid was eventually to stand some 146 metres (nearly 480 feet) high, the equivalent of a modern tower-block over fifty storeys tall, and to incorporate over two million blocks of stone, few of which would have weighed less than a ton and many of which would have weighed considerably more. It has been estimated that some of the lower casing stones may have weighed as much as fifteen tons.

It can be hard to envisage such a vast structure; the claim that the base of the Great Pyramid could comfortably accommodate both the Houses of Parliament and St Paul's Cathedral may perhaps help. Napoleon Bonaparte, an enthusiastic student of Egypt's antiquity, was so impressed by his visit to Giza that he himself (assisted by his mathematician) announced that there was enough stone in the three Giza Pyramids to build a wall three metres (ten feet) high all around France.

The Great Pyramid is the most precisely aligned of all the pyramids. Orientation was clearly important to the surveyors. Whether this accuracy was a practical response to the Dahshur and Meidum disasters, or a religious need to ensure the exact alignment of the burial chamber (and therefore the dead king), we cannot now be certain. However, the end result is in no doubt. The sides of Khufu's pyramid are oriented almost exactly to true north while the subsequent neighbouring pyramids, built by Khufu's son and grandson, would be closely aligned both with each other and with elements of the Great Pyramid complex. The base of Khufu's pyramid is almost completely level, while the length of the sides varies by less than five centimetres (two inches).

Inside and beneath the pyramid is a warren of passages and rooms. At first sight it appears that the architect, in time-honoured fashion, underwent several changes of mind as the burial chamber moved from below ground (the unfinished "Subterranean Chamber" carved out of the bedrock) first to the middle of the pyramid (the almost completed limestone "Queen's Chamber") and finally to a position high within the body of the pyramid (the red granite "King's Chamber"). Here Khufu was to be entombed in his sarcophagus of red Aswan granite for all eternity. However, some Egyptologists believe that all three chambers were a part of the original plan, with the "Queen's Chamber" designed to act as a *serdab* room, holding a statue of the deceased king which could serve as a substitute body. Above the King's Chamber were built five stress-relieving chambers, an innovation that spread the load of the pyramid which would otherwise put intolerable weight and stress on the ceiling of the burial chamber. "Airshafts," oriented towards the northern Pole star, led from the King's and the Queen's Chambers through the body of the pyramid; these may well have originally been blocked by the outer casing and their purpose is, as yet, not fully understood—although it seems likely to have been of a ritual rather than a practical nature.

Khufu, all too well aware that his tomb would attract thieves, intended his last resting place to be well protected. He provided three stone portcullises to block the entrance to his burial chamber, and ensured that the narrow ascending entrance passageway would be sealed with massive blocks of stone, stored before use in the purpose-built Grand Gallery. He did not, however, intend that those who sealed his tomb should themselves be entombed; images of loyal priests and slaves dying alongside pharaoh's mummy are once again the product of vivid Hollywood imaginations. Khufu's men were provided with an escape route. A narrow shaft led downwards from the top of the ascending passageway to the lower or descending passage which led to the Subterranean Chamber. Climbing up the descending passageway, the tomb builders could emerge through the original pyramid entrance 16.5 metres (50 feet) up the north face. This could then be blocked and covered with the limestone casing which would make it—or so it was hoped—impossible to detect.

Unfortunately, the robbers were not fooled, and Khufu was disturbed from his rest before the end of the Old Kingdom. Blocks from his pyramid complex were already being re-used a mere five and a half centuries after his death, when they started to appear in the Middle Kingdom pyramid of

Amenemhat I. The pyramid itself survived more or less intact throughout the dynastic age but eventually the white limestone outer casing was stripped, with much of it being used to build the medieval city of Cairo.

Khufu's pyramid was originally surrounded by a paved courtyard enclosed within a tall limestone wall; following the Meidum plan, access to this inner area was via the causeway which led upwards from the valley temple to the large mortuary temple. Today little of this grandeur remains, but when Herodotus visited Giza the causeway was substantially intact, allowing tourists to walk through the gloom of the passageway to reach the shining brilliance of the pyramid itself. Herodotus was clearly impressed: "This causeway is five furlongs in length, ten fathoms wide, and in height, at its highest part, eight fathoms. It is built of polished stone, and is covered with the carvings of animals." (*Histories, Book 2*: 124.)

Outside the enclosure wall were built one small satellite pyramid—a pyramid, reminiscent of the southern tomb in Djoser's complex, intended somehow for the use of the dead king—and three larger queen's pyramids. These were provided for the burials of the king's most immediate female relatives. Here Herodotus again has a tale to tell, a tale that perhaps puts his accuracy as a reporter into serious doubt:

> So wicked was Cheops that, when he had spent all his treasure and needed more, he sent his daughter to work in a brothel, ordering her to earn him a certain sum; how much, I was never told. This she managed to do. However, at the same time, having decided to build a monument to her own memory, she asked each client to give her a stone. With these stones she built the middle pyramid of the three that stand in front of the Great Pyramid.
>
> *Histories,* Book 2: 126

Queen Hetepheres, almost certainly the mother of Khufu, was probably honoured with the most northerly of these three pyramids. Chance has ensured that Hetepheres has become one of the few female characters to emerge from the obscurity of Old Kingdom history. In 1925 the leg of a photographic tripod, positioned close to the northerly queen's pyramid, sank deep into the desert sand. This accident led to the discovery of a blocked shaft leading to a simple chamber. Here, neatly packed, were the remains of Hetepheres' burial equipment plus her empty alabaster sarcophagus and her canopic chest complete with preserved internal organs. The burial equipment included a dismantled canopy or tent, two sitting chairs and one carrying chair. The wooden elements of these pieces had long since rotted away, but enough clues remained for the archaeologists to reconstruct the queen's furniture with a fair degree of accuracy. More private items found in the store included gold razors and knives, small alabaster pots containing perfumes and kohl and a collection of jewellery including silver bracelets and anklets. These items are today displayed in Cairo Museum. While it is impossible to reconstruct the chain of events following Hetepheres' funeral with absolute certainty this collection, incomplete, damaged and lacking a body yet including entrails, clearly represents the hidden remains of a robbed royal burial.

Her son Khufu ensured that he was well provided with boats, both real and symbolic. Five boat-shaped but empty pits were excavated close to the causeway and mortuary temple, outside his pyramid enclosure wall. The significance of these phantom boats is nowhere explained, but as the pyramid functioned as a symbolic port, the point of departure for the Afterlife, they may have been intended to allow the dead king to sail to his destiny alongside Re. In contrast, two narrow rectangular pits dug parallel to the south side of the pyramid were found to house actual, dismantled, boats. While one boat remains the subject of a conservation project the other has been fully reassembled and is now housed in its own museum alongside the pyramid. Made out of cedar planks sewn together with fibre ropes, the full-sized boat is a wooden copy of a papyrus reed boat, complete with cabin and five oars on either side. Whether this represents a boat to be used after death, a boat that was actually used during the king's lifetime or even a boat used during the royal funeral, we do not know.

The Great Pyramid was never intended to stand alone. Proximity in death to the pharaoh was considered a great privilege, and we find all Old Kingdom royal tombs surrounded by the graves of the courtiers who perhaps hoped to share some of the after-life experiences of their dead king. To threaten to withdraw the privilege of burial in the royal necrop-

olis—a threat used occasionally by pharaohs to reinforce their decrees—
was to threaten the prospect of eternal life itself. Giza is no exception to
this rule, and here we find the attendant graves sorted into different
groups. To the east of the Great Pyramid stood the mastaba tombs of the
royal family and to the west the mastabas of Khufu's courtiers, all
arranged tidily in neat, parallel streets. Buried below the desert sands
just outside the royal necropolis were the less ornate tombs of the workers who toiled to build the pyramids. The significance of their graves will
be explored further in Chapter 3.

> Cheops reigned, or so the Egyptians say, some fifty years. He
> was succeeded at his demise by Chephren, his brother. Cheph-
> ren followed his predecessor's conduct, and like him built a
> pyramid which did not, however, equal his brother's in size. Of
> this I am certain, for I measured them both myself.... Cheph-
> ren's reign lasted fifty-six years, and so Egypt suffered for a total
> of one hundred and six years, during which time the temples
> remained closed. The Egyptians so detest the memory of these
> kings that they never even speak their names.
>
> *Histories*, Book 2: 127–8

Khufu's pyramid was effectively complete at his death. However, he
had been lucky enough to be blessed with an exceptionally long reign.
His son and immediate successor, Djedefre, was considerably less ambitious. At Abu Roash, some eight kilometres (five miles) from Giza, he
started to build a pyramid with an old-fashioned subterranean burial
chamber, but work on his project ground to a halt with the death of the
king. Today Abu Roash is the site of a modern industrial complex, its
pyramid a shapeless, low mound. Djedefre was followed on the throne
by his brother Khaefre (Chephren to Herodotus), and he in turn by his
son, Menkaure. Both these kings returned to the Giza plateau, where they
built alongside the Great Pyramid.

Khaefre's pyramid, actually some three metres (ten feet) lower than that
of Khufu, is built on higher ground which offers the illusion that it is the
larger monument. Today Khaefre's pyramid is the only one of the three to

retain some of its original white casing and this, although slightly tarnished by age and pollution, allows us a glimpse of how the pyramids might once have shone in the sunlight. With Khaefre's reign came great advances in sculpture, so that although many of his statues were recycled in antiquity, we have several images of this confident, powerful monarch. However, it is as the face of the sphinx that Khaefre is best recognized. The sphinx, with its lion body and human head suggesting the combined symbols of kingship and the sun, was carved from the natural rock to stand guard alongside Khaefre's pyramid causeway.

Khaefre's pyramid was to be the last of the great pyramids. His son and heir, Menkaure, was happy to build on an altogether smaller scale; his pyramid is about a tenth by mass of his grandfather's and stands only 66 metres (about 216 feet) high. While we are offered no explanation for this sudden reduction in size, there are several possible reasons. It may be that, with many of the royal craftsmen now engaged in the building of temples and the carving of statues, Menkaure's resources were already stretched; the building of five substantial pyramids over the preceding four reigns would certainly have drained the royal coffers. Also, Menkaure may not have actually felt the need for a large pyramid. A shift in the theology of death at this time seems to have decreed that temples rather than tombs become the buildings of importance, and indeed Menkaure's mortuary temple is relatively large compared to his pyramid. It is important that we do not inflict our own modern prejudices—the bigger the pyramid, the better—on Menkaure.

More prosaically, it may be that the Giza Plateau was getting crowded, or that the king doubted his own longevity and decided to err on the side of caution. In the words of Egyptologist Toby Wilkinson, it seems that an important lesson was already being learned: "An unfinished pyramid is absolutely no use at all if you are an Egyptian king, and so perhaps the lesson that was learned over the generations was that unless you came to the throne at a young age it was safer to begin a much smaller pyramid in the secure knowledge that you might finish it before your death, and therefore it would be effective for you in the Afterlife."

Whatever Menkaure's reasoning, time proved his decision to have been the right one. Although he reigned for at least twenty-six years, the king's small-scale pyramid complex remained unfinished at his death—at which point it had to be completed, somewhat ignominiously, in mud brick. Although his tomb was robbed in antiquity, Menkaure's body was restored and reinterred in a new coffin during the Late Period Saite era. Later, the king again attracted thieves. Today Menkaure is represented by a pair of mummified legs, a foot and a segment of torso housed in the British Museum.

Pyramid building was to continue on a reduced scale throughout the Old and Middle Kingdoms, with small private pyramids playing a part in the funerary architecture of the New Kingdom, and Nubian pyramids emerging during the Third Intermediate Period. None of these later pyramids, however, was to approach the grandeur and sheer architectural skill of the Giza monuments. The Great Pyramid, the only surviving member of the seven wonders of the ancient world, today stands as a tribute not only to Khufu, but to the social organization of Old Kingdom Egypt.

CHAPTER THREE

Who?
The Lost City

> This is reconstructing history. When we write about this in the
> history books and the archaeology books it will be the most im-
> portant chapter in those books because it tells us for the first time
> about the majority of the Egyptians, the farmers and the work-
> men, who were involved in the construction of the pyramids.
>
> Zahi Hawass, chief archaeologist of the Giza Plateau

AS WE HAVE SEEN, THE HISTORY OF THE GREAT ROYAL PYRAMID BUILDERS, OF
Djoser, Snefru, Khufu and Khaefre, is tolerably well understood. However,
these kings were not in any practical sense the real "pyramid builders" of
Egypt, and the extent to which they had any hands-on involvement in the
design and construction of their tombs must be open to doubt. Egyptology has, by tradition, concentrated on the written, the royal and the monumental at the expense of the ordinary and down-to-earth, and the middle-
or working-class man or woman is still regrettably absent from Egypt's long

history. While this bias is now being recognized and corrected, it has had a lingering effect on pyramid studies.

Lack of evidence—evidence which for many years no one sought to discover—has led to a regrettable tendency to take pyramids out of their context, to examine them as isolated, theoretical monuments somehow unconnected with daily life in the Nile Valley. Indeed, some have taken things a stage further, by suggesting that the pyramids were actually built by non-human extraterrestrials! And yet the Great Pyramid itself preserves the image of its makers, for captured within its stones and mortar are the charcoal and pottery fragments, the scraps of broken tools, the chisel marks and even the graffiti which make obvious its human origins. To Egyptologist and pyramid expert Mark Lehner this is the human fabric, the software, of the pyramids.

But who were these pyramid builders? Herodotus would have us believe that they were a band of one hundred thousand slaves, forced to work for twenty or thirty years against their will. But this image of mass slavery, so appealing to film makers, does not quite fit with our understanding of Old Kingdom society. There is no doubt that there were slaves in ancient Egypt nor, indeed, that during the New Kingdom slaves were being used on royal building projects. Ramesses II would have been unable to complete his impressive Nubian temples without the "help" of prisoners-of-war captured to order from the neighbouring oases. But throughout the Old Kingdom state-owned slaves were a negligible proportion of the population; Herodotus' hundred thousand would have been a substantial 5–10 percent and it seems impossible that such large-scale slavery would have gone undetected by archaeologists and historians, or unmentioned in the contemporary literature.

It may be that this conflict of evidence is merely a problem of definition. Herodotus, a Greek, would have been accustomed to the idea of large-scale slavery—the slave, in his experience, being a well-defined member of the community. Egypt, in contrast, used a wide variety of terms to describe those at the very bottom of her social pyramid. The modern word "slave" is almost certainly too crude a term to use when considering the Egyptian un-free, many of whom should probably be reclassified in our own terms as serfs, tied-peasants, prisoners-or-war or even servants rather than slaves. But if the pyramid workforce was not made up of classic, totally subjugated slaves, who could they have been? Did pharaoh force people to work on his project, did they volunteer, or were they paid? For the moment, while we consider the archaeological evidence, we will simply classify them as workers.

Herodotus' numbers, too, fail to stand up to close scrutiny. Egypt lacked sophisticated stone-cutting and lifting machinery, and so it is obvious that a substantial workforce would have been required to build a massive stone monument. But Herodotus' estimate of one hundred thousand permanent labourers has always seemed far too high. One hundred thousand is just slightly higher than the population of Cambridge, Massachusetts, or just slightly lower than the population of Cambridge, England. The management of such vast numbers would have been a logistical nightmare while the workers' camp, or village, would have been absolutely enormous with a suitably large cemetery attached. Simply feeding one hundred thousand would be difficult.

We know that later in their history the Egyptians established a tradition of calling up temporary manual workers to work in shifts on state projects; could this be what was happening at Giza? Herodotus' figure certainly appears far more acceptable if it is broken down into three-monthly shifts of twenty-five thousand men and, indeed, this is approximately the number of labourers that many Egyptologists, having made their own calculations based on estimated work-rates, would have expected to find on site.

So far, however, our revision of Herodotus has been entirely based on theory. In order to confirm the exact status of the workers, and to approximate their numbers, archaeologists knew that they must find the homes and graves of the pyramid builders—the so-called "Lost City of the Pyramids." While it was possible that the workforce had been accommodated on the Nile floodplain—and therefore that their site had vanished for ever—it seemed more likely that they would have lived on the plateau, not too far away from their work.

Egypt's builders did not commute, they lived on site for the duration of their work. All the great Egyptian state building projects were provided with workers' accommodation. Here, in reasonable comfort, lived the permanent, salaried officials connected with the project: the supervisors, scribes, priests and guards plus their support staff of bakers, toolmakers, laundrymen and others and, of course, their wives, children, dependants, servants, livestock and pets. Here, too, the king might establish a fully staffed residence, complete with throne room and harem quarters, which would allow him and his retinue to inspect his monument in comfort. The tradition of building in mud-brick meant that a palace could be built from scratch with surprising ease; indeed, we are told that the New Kingdom Pharaoh Akhenaten was able to build an entire city in less than four years. Additional accommodation, possibly of a less sophisticated and more temporary nature, and perhaps slightly removed from the élite worker housing, would be needed for the manual labourers.

The best-known example of this form of tied accommodation is probably the New Kingdom workmen's village of Deir el-Medina, a permanent state-owned housing complex which became home to generations of workmen employed to cut the tombs in the Valley of the Kings. This well-preserved village has yielded both archaeological and textual data which allows us to recreate the lives of its residents. As the rock-cut tomb was a constricted, confined workplace, there was no need to employ the vast numbers of manual labourers who would be needed on a pyramid site; everyone who worked in the Valley was therefore classed as an élite artisan and accommodated accordingly. The workmen lived in the village with their wives, families and dependants, separated from the daily life of nearby Thebes. When working their weekly shifts in the Valley they lodged in temporary, all-male accommodation close by the tomb.

The Middle Kingdom pyramid necropolis of Illahun, situated at the mouth of the Faiyum, was built some eight hundred years after Khufu's pyramid yet hints at the type of situation that might be expected at Giza. Here, close by the ruins of the valley temple of the pyramid of Senwosret II, lie the remains of what was once a substantial walled pyramid town with a population estimated at nine or ten thousand. This was made up of the administrators and priests who ran the pyramid complex, plus the permanent workers employed in its construction. Illahun (sometimes called Kahun) shows deliberate town planning and rigid social stratification. To the north-east are nine or ten large estates, the residences of the highest ranking necropolis officials, while to the south-west lie the more humble homes of the permanent pyramid employees, arranged in neat rows. No accommodation for a more temporary workforce has yet been discovered, and there is always the possibility that this has been lost beneath the modern cultivation that has encroached upon the town.

The large Illahun estates were the height of Middle Kingdom luxury: spacious, porticoed and provided with shady gardens where hot and dusty officials could relax after a hard day at the pyramid. However, the estates were more than family homes; each served as an independent economic unit, with its own huge granary. These granaries could, together, produce enough bread to feed the entire population of Illahun. Egypt had no money; her wages and taxes were paid in man-hours and in kind. The granaries at Illahun suggest that the large estates were actually payment mechanisms financed by the treasury; that they provided the workforce with grain, and probably other foods, in return for their services at the pyramid site.

Behind Khaefre's pyramid runs a series of long galleries. Flinders Petrie, surveying the Giza Plateau in 1880–82, believed that these were the remains of the barracks provided to house the pyramid workers. He calculated that this rather basic accommodation would hold some four thousand men. However, Petrie was unable to carry out any detailed excavation in his "barracks." Recent excavations have made obvious the complete absence of the settlement debris that we would normally expect to find in the ruins of long-term living accommodation, and it is now generally accepted that the galleries are more likely to have been workshops or storerooms connected with the pyramid cult.

In the early twentieth century George Reisner was to excavate a series of rather run-down Old Kingdom mud-brick houses in the area around the valley temple of Menkaure. These were not, however, the houses of the pyramid workers but the homes of those who continued to serve the cult of the dead king after the Giza building projects had ended.

Of more relevance to our quest for the pyramid builders is the evidence uncovered in the Cairo suburb of Nazlet el-Samman, a modern village at the foot of the Giza Plateau. The presence of the village makes large-scale excavation in this area impossible, and it is only when local building projects are undertaken that Egyptologists are offered a tantalizing glimpse of the remains hidden beneath the desert sands. In the late 1980s improvements to Cairo's sewerage system involved the taking of borings and the cutting of trenches to the east of the pyramids, with the main trench passing directly over the remains of Khufu's valley temple. Within the trench archaeologists, working in conjunction with the contractors, were able to see clear evidence of intensive Old Kingdom oc-cupation—mud-brick buildings, thousands of potsherds including red burnished ware, animal bones with butchery marks, ash and even part of a thick mud-brick wall which must have belonged to a substantial build-ing, possibly even a palace. The trench was, however, filled in and this region—a prime candidate for the title of "lost city of the pyramid builders"—is as yet unexcavated.

To the south of the Sphinx and to the west of the modern village runs an ancient limestone wall known in Arabic as the "Wall of the Crow." This wall, with its imposing gateway, seems to have served as the official en-trance to the Old Kingdom necropolis. By passing through the gate, priests, officials, workmen and kings would have moved from the land of the liv-ing to the pyramid land of the dead. Here, in 1988–89, excavation by Mark Lehner had revealed a large rectangular building filled with curious pedestals. It was initially classified as a granary equipped with pedestals to support grain silos, until the subsequent discovery of seal impressions referring to the "wabet." This term literally translates as "the thing that is pure," but it was commonly used to cover both the embalming workshop and all the institutions connected with the supply of funerary goods. This suggests that this building might actually have been a storehouse. Then, in 1990, a mechanical digger collecting sand for a local building project uncovered mud-brick walls and massive quantities of pottery including many broken bread-moulds. Work stopped immediately, and a team of ar-chaeologists, again led by Mark Lehner, moved in.

The digger had uncovered part of what was to prove to be a large com-plex of mud-brick buildings dating to the time of the pyramid builders. However, although there was some evidence of domestic housing, this was no ordinary pyramid town. As Mark Lehner recalls: "We have seen things here that look like workers' houses, but most of what we are finding looks as though it is geared towards production."

Thick, heavy bread, made with emmer wheat or barley, was a staple of the Egyptian diet. Not only was it a major food, it was also the principal ingredient of the rather weak but highly nutritious beer that was the usual daily drink. In any pyramid town or city we would expect to find bread-processing facilities, with a brewery close by. Now hundreds of thick, bell-shaped, pottery bread-moulds marked the site of two bakeries. Here was evidence of bread production on a truly vast scale. There were the vats where the dough would have been mixed, the moulds themselves, and the baking pits where the filled moulds—placed two together to form a double cone shape and then held upright in sockets somewhat reminiscent of modern egg-boxes—would have been cooked in the ash and hot embers. Ovens, used to bake domestic bread, were evidently not used for production on such a massive scale. As yet no grain-processing area has been discovered and, although a large area remains to be excavated, it may be that this essential component of bread was being taken to Giza already prepared.

Next door to the bakeries the archaeologists uncovered a large building equipped with a curious series of ankle-height "benches," either shelves or architectural features interspaced by troughs. The floor of this building was covered by a thick deposit of hardened ash and organic material including fragile fish remains. By consolidating the deposit, and then scraping at it with a penknife, it proved possible to separate out and identify gills, fins, heads and even bones. Microscopic analysis later showed that the deposits in the troughs between the benches were full of crushed and broken fish bone. It seemed that the team had discovered a fish-processing unit.

As we have already seen, each year the retreating Nile floodwaters left behind numerous fish, stranded in the catchment basins. This generous protein harvest was much appreciated, and tomb scenes show the fish being scaled, gutted and then dried with the head and gills still in place. Treated in this way the fish, perhaps somewhat similar in taste to modern Bombay ducks, or the Egyptian dried, salted fish known as *farseekh*, would last for many months. However, the bones recovered from the Giza fishery included gills and fins, the parts that archaeologists would normally expect to find at the eating site rather than the processing unit. Either the

Giza fish were being preserved to a different recipe, perhaps being both dried and smoked or salted without their head and gills, or fish were being both processed and consumed within this building.

We might have anticipated that the non-élite pyramid builders were fed on a diet of bread and fish, perhaps supplemented by vegetables; these, the least expensive of foods, would provide enough carbohydrates, protein and beer to fuel a workforce made hungry and thirsty by vigorous manual labour. Herodotus, ever helpful, even provides us with details of the menu offered to his pyramid-building slaves:

> There is an inscription in Egyptian writing on the pyramid which records the quantity of radishes, onions and garlic eaten by the labourers who built it, and I remember very well that the interpreter who read the inscription to me said that the money spent in this way was the equivalent of sixteen hundred talents of silver. If this is indeed a true record, what a vast sum must have been spent on iron tools used in the work, and on the feeding and clothing of the labourers, considering the length of time that the project lasted.
>
> *Histories,* Book 2: 125

Herodotus, correct in his assumption that pyramid building was an expensive business, did not realize that the ancient Egyptians had no access to iron tools. By now the archaeologists, too, were coming to the conclusion that they were investigating an expensive site. The Giza workers were obviously producing a great deal of wood ash in their baking, in their fishery and in their copper workshops, the evidence for which is just starting to appear. This ash lingers today to choke the Egyptologists as they work. This is curious. Egypt, as we have already seen, is a country of few trees and intensive wood burning is the sign, not of a slave compound, but of a wealthy community.

Wet filtration allows archaeologists to examine the debris and detritus of the past. By putting dirt, sand or soil into water and then sieving it through a series of meshes of ever-increasing fineness, it is possible to separate and grade the sediment which can then be dried in the sun, and

sorted. At Giza this technique has been used to recover ancient plant remains, small or broken animal bones and even small mud seals that have
occasionally yield the name of a long-dead worker. The grains recovered
in this way have suggested that the bakers were working with barley to
produce a heavy, dark bread. Most of the animal bones recovered—more
fish, duck and the occasional sheep and pig—are what we might expect
to find at a settlement site. Totally unexpected, however, are the remains
of many choice cuts of prime meat less than two years old.

Throughout the dynastic age cattle were an expensive luxury, far beyond the reach of the ordinary worker who might hope to keep his own
geese, and maybe even a sheep or pig, but never a cow. Cows, unlike pigs,
are not village animals and they cannot subsist off household scraps. These
newly discovered cattle could not have been raised among the housing
and industrial units of the pyramid city and must have been imported live,
most probably from the Delta, and then butchered at Giza. Who was send-
ing this meat to the pyramids? It may have come from the king's own extensive estates, but it is more likely to have come from the estates owned
by the pyramid complex itself.

As we have already seen, the pyramid was not intended merely to act
as a tomb—any simple grave could have served that purpose. Each pyramid complex was intended to function as a permanent cult centre whose
priest would make offerings for all eternity to the dead king. This was important. Without the offerings, the royal soul might starve, die of thirst or
be forgotten. Each pyramid was therefore granted one or more endowments of land complete with farms, peasants and livestock which would
generate sufficient income—in the form of goods, labour and produce
rather than money—to fund the priests who would perform the necessary
daily rituals for ever.

This land was not necessarily close to the pyramid itself; while there
were many pyramid estates in the fertile Delta farmland the thirty-five estates endowed by Snefru and listed in the valley temple of his Bent Pyramid were mainly sited in Middle Egypt. Produce from the pyramid estate
would be sent to the pyramid complex where, having first been offered to
the divine departed, it would then be redistributed among the priests and
pyramid staff. In theory, this system ensured that the pyramid cult would

survive for ever. In practice, it ensured that the cults lasted until the First Intermediate Period when the pyramid estates were gradually fragmented and lack of funding caused the pyramid complex to fall into disuse. A similar system of endowments was used to fund the Ka-priests who offered to the souls of Egypt's non-royal dead and, by the end of the Old Kingdom, was also used to fund the temples.

We do not know who was eating the bread, fish and meat discovered at Giza. However, it seems highly likely that some, if not all, of the food was eventually being consumed by the pyramid builders. Did everyone share the meat—even the manual labourers? Was it reserved for the élite workers? Can the presence of prestige food even be taken as confirmation of a royal residence attached to the pyramid city? Parallels with Illahun would suggest that we might expect to find the Giza workers being provisioned by a series of estates—maybe even including a palace—operating within the pyramid city.

A chance discovery in the dunes above and to the west of the industrial complex has helped to confirm its identification with the pyramid builders. Here, one day, a horse carrying a lady stumbled, its leg exposing a fragment of mud-brick wall. This proved to be part of an ancient tomb, itself part of an extensive non-royal cemetery that yielded Old Kingdom pottery dating to the 4th and 5th Dynasties. Zahi Hawass, the excavator of the cemetery, has so far uncovered over six hundred burials arranged on two levels. The lower level contains the simpler tombs and graves, although there is also an assortment of miniature step-pyramids, small-scale mastabas and beehive-shaped tombs, some of which incorporate stone elements—Aswan granite, Tura limestone and black basalt—"liberated" from the pyramid complex or perhaps even donated by a grateful king. Higher up the slope are larger and more sophisticated limestone tombs and a serdab housing four statues. The experts working on pharaoh's tomb were obviously able to put their skills—or their subordinates' skills—to good use, and had made elaborate preparations for an eternity spent lying close to their king.

On the basis of the evidence from the tombs, from the unexcavated Nazlet el-Samman settlement site and from the industrial complex below the cemetery Zahi Hawass has estimated that Giza would have been home to approximately five thousand permanent élite workers (officials, supervisors and master-craftsmen) plus fifteen thousand temporary manual workers. The total number working at the site at any given time would be no higher than twenty thousand. Inscriptions within the more sophisticated limestone tombs make clear the organization of the manual workers. Initially they were divided into crews of approximately two thousand. These crews were then subdivided into named gangs of one thousand and the gangs further split into five groups or phyles of approximately two hundred. The phyles then broke down into divisions, so that what had started out as a large body of workers was ultimately reduced to a series of small, easily controlled units of maybe twenty workers.

As the manual labourers were likely to have been a temporary workforce, possibly housed in a temporary camp close by the permanent settlement at Nazlet el-Samman, their burials represent the unfortunate few who died while working their shift. Some of these workers were buried with the flint and stone tools of their trade. The élite, full- or part-time salaried necropolis employees would have expected to live and possibly die at the site until the pyramid complex was complete. Their more substantial tombs have yielded evidence that links them directly with the food production centre below. One, for example, appears to be the tomb of the master baker and his family, and the wall of his tomb shows scenes of bread and beer production. Other tombs belonged to the important officials closely involved in the building of the pyramid itself; here we find the remains of the pyramid architects, sculptors and overseers.

Their relative simplicity, their lack of precious gold and jewellery, and their dense covering of dry sand had ensured that the tombs remained intact, their skeletons and basic grave goods undisturbed by robbers and uncontaminated by modern pollutants. Archaeologists and scientists have therefore been able to use the skeletons to build up a profile of those who lived and died at Giza. By comparing the bones from the workers' cemetery with bones recovered fifty years earlier from the "tombs of the nobles," the substantial mastaba tombs built by Egypt's élite alongside the pyramids, this profile may be extended to encompass the whole of Old Kingdom society.

As Professor Fawzia Hussein, of the Department of Human Genetics, Cairo University, has explained, the potential of such a collection is enormous: "You can squeeze many, many facts about their lives and how they looked during their life. This is our aim. When they died, were they young? We can think about when they die, we can think about their workload; there are many things which can be squeezed from the bones."

So far this work is still in progress; it will not be completed until the last skeleton has been excavated and examined. However, the evidence that has already emerged is helping to confirm our theoretical interpretation of life in an ancient pyramid city.

The first step has been to sort the bones by sex and by age, paying particular attention to the evidence provided by the teeth, the pelvis and the skull. Of the six hundred-plus skeletons so far analysed from the workmen's graves, half are male and half are female, with children and babies making up over 23 percent of the cemetery population. This mixed population agrees well with the impression of life at an ancient construction site already gleaned from Deir el-Medina and Illahun; far from being occupied by teams of male slaves, the pyramid city—if not the temporary camp—had been home to families including babies. Subsequent analysis of DNA—the chemical substance that carries genetic information from one generation to the next—by Dr Moamina Kamal of Cairo University Medical School confirmed that these were indeed family units, with the DNA of the adult bones correlating closely to that of the children.

Some of the skeletons showed signs of ancient, mended fractures. That the workmen should suffer the occasional crushed or broken limb comes as no great surprise; conditions on the building site, where massive blocks were being manoeuvred quickly and without the benefit of modern machinery, would have been hazardous to say the least, and we may imagine that serious accidents happened with depressing frequency. The skill of the Egyptian doctors was, by the New Kingdom, famed throughout the ancient world; foreign rulers afflicted with rare complaints were wont to write to pharaoh, demanding the services of his physicians.

We know from texts written a thousand years after the pyramid age that these doctors understood the best method of treating a fracture. We are told that the damaged limb was to be straightened and properly aligned, and the wound coated with honey and an unknown mineral before splinting and then bandaging for maybe up to a month. Evidence that this or a similar splinting treatment was being used during the Old Kingdom had already been recovered from the tombs of the nobles. Now here, in the tombs of the pyramid builders, was proof that this high standard of medical care was being extended throughout the entire Giza community. Either the workmen had access to a competent doctor, or everyone in the community knew how to mend a broken limb.

Even more impressive is the evidence that one of the workers had survived the amputation—either deliberate of accidental, we cannot tell which—of an arm. Amputation under primitive surgical conditions carries a serious risk of excessive blood loss and uncontrolled infection, both of which can prove fatal. Here, however, the wound had healed well. Again, a similar situation has been found among the noble bones, with one unfortunate individual surviving the amputation of a leg. Nevertheless, despite this evidence of good quality medical care, examination of the two communities shows that the worker men and women died on average ten years earlier than their noble contemporaries, who survived to an average age of forty to forty-five. We might, to a certain extent, expect this; it seems likely that the worker population was selected on the basis of their ability to perform hard physical labour and was therefore unlikely to include many elderly men. Nevertheless, it seems that Egypt's nobles, by eating the best foods and avoiding the hazards of manual labour, the bilharzia-infected Nile and the cramped lower-class living conditions which encouraged the spread of disease, were able to extend their lifespan by an impressive 25 percent.

The difference in worker/noble health is highlighted by an examination of the vertebrae. Some of the worker backbones show distinctive signs of stress and compression leading to spinal curvature which, in a few individuals, would have been quite pronounced. The cause of this stress is as yet unproven, although various suggestions have been put forward, ranging from the effects of a lifetime of manual work to an unidentified genetic disorder affecting the spine. It may be that a combination of these factors is involved; juvenile kyphosis, a curvature of the spine identified in 1920 by a German doctor studying a group of young agricultural workers involved in heavy labour, was felt to be caused by mechanical factors plus a genetic predisposition.

The fact that the curvature is found in both sexes may perhaps indicate that it is not just the direct result of working on the pyramid site, as there is no other evidence to suggest that the women whom we know to have been living in the pyramid city were actually employed as construction workers. Absence of evidence is not, of course, evidence of absence, but the ancient Egyptians, who allowed their women a legal independence rarely seen until modern times, were very traditional in their domestic arrangements. The married woman, the "Mistress of the House," was free to work outside the home, but she was expected to put her household duties first. Hers was very much an indoor world—a time-consuming world of child care, food and drink preparation, laundry and clothing—in contrast to the more outdoor, independent life of her husband.

If we take as a parallel the New Kingdom necropolis village of Deir el-Medina we might expect to find that, although the élite workers lived in the village, or the pyramid city, with their wives and families, the women stuck to their traditional duties and were not expected to intrude on the male work gangs. For some of these women, hard physical work would in any case have been impossible as they were pregnant. Problems of pregnancy and labour cut across the social divide, defeating the Old Kingdom doctors. In both the worker and the noble populations at Giza the women died younger than their menfolk, with many not reaching the age of thirty. Several are known to have died in childbirth, with the most remarkable case being that of a dwarf lady from the worker community, who died attempting to deliver a normal-sized baby through her abnormally narrow pelvis.

If the élite workers, professional civil servants, were unlikely to live in anything other than traditional family units, what about the temporary workers? Could they have included women among their numbers? We will return to this question in Chapter 5.

Work on the Giza plateau, and in the Cairo laboratories, will continue for many years. Already, however, enough evidence has emerged to allow us to reconstruct the lives of the pyramid builders with a fair degree of confidence. The deep-rooted idea of permanent large-scale slave labour must be abandoned. It seems that the pyramids were built by a permanent workforce of some five thousand skilled technicians, government employees who lived with their families on site throughout the entire building programme. Their "pyramid city" was divided into at least two distinct zones: the mud-brick houses were most probably built close to the valley temple of Khufu, while the processing area, or industrial complex, which supported the workers was further to the south. There may even have been a royal residence within the pyramid city. The workers built their tombs above the pyramid city, close to the king's pyramid yet outside the pyramid boundary wall. The élite workers were supplemented by approximately fifteen thousand manual labourers who arrived at the site, worked a lengthy shift, and then returned home. A few unfortunates died on site, and they too were buried on the outskirts of the pyramid city.

A large workforce would require efficient administration. As yet we have no understanding of the system for paying rations, although it is clear that the workforce would have had to be fed. Already there is evidence of food production on a massive scale and proof that some, at least, of the Giza residents were eating a high quality diet of meat, bread and fish. We might reasonably expect the discovery of storage facilities, perhaps even warehouses, to follow. The presence of the government employees in the pyramid city is easy for us to understand. But who were the unskilled people who turned up to work the manual shifts? And exactly how many were there? In order to expand the information obtained by excavation, we now need to consider the actual process of pyramid building.

ABOVE: Sunset over the Nile. (*Richard Reisz*)

BELOW: The Sphinx and the Great Pyramid of Khufu beyond. (*Richard Reisz*)

LEFT: The magnificent and imposing Luxor Temple at Thebes. (*Richard Reisz*)

BELOW LEFT: Luxor Temple. (*Richard Reisz*)

RIGHT: The Bent Pyramid of the 4th Dynasty pharaoh Snefru at Dahshur. (*Hamish Niven*)

BELOW RIGHT: Khaefre's pyramid at Giza, showing the remains of the original casing on the pinnacle. (*Richard Reisz*)

ABOVE: The excavations below the site of the Giza pyramids. (Hamish Niven)

RIGHT: Djoser's step-pyramid at Sakkara: Egypt's first stone monument. (Richard Reisz)

ABOVE: The great Karnak temple of Amen at Thebes. (*Hamish Niven*)

LEFT: The mighty columns of the Karnak temple. (*Hamish Niven*)

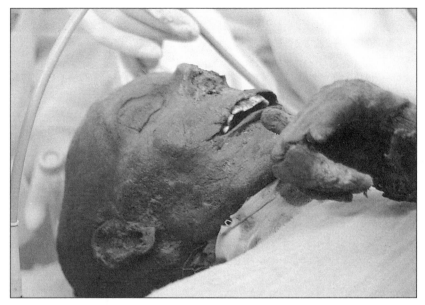

ABOVE: Taking a DNA sample from the mummy of Tuthmosis III. (*Richard Reisz*) .

BELOW: The foot of Tuthmosis III: the prints are still intact on the toes. (*Richard Reisz*)

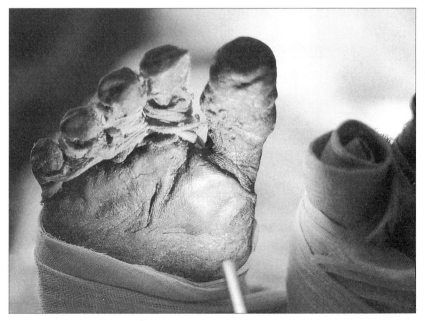

ABOVE: View of Amarna. *(Richard Reisz)*

BELOW: Boundary stela at Amarna. *(Richard Reisz)*

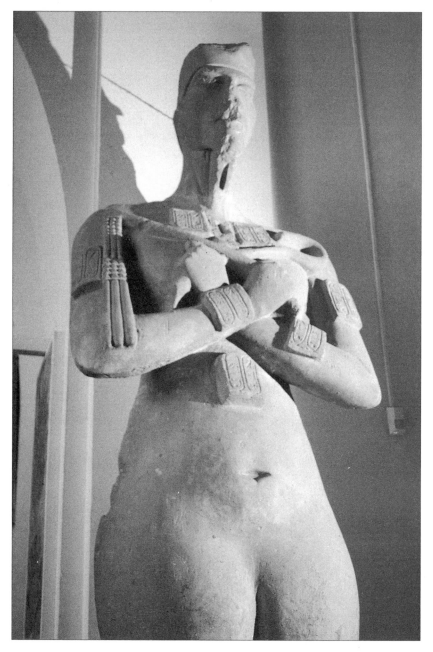

ABOVE: The asexual statue of Akhenaten which has caused much speculation among Egyptologists: was this representation of the 'heretic king' the result of a revolutionary art style or the realistic depiction of a man afflicted with a hereditary, deforming disease? (*Richard Reisz*)

CHAPTER FOUR

How?
The Building
of the Pyramids

> We believe that the Egyptians were like you and me. They were
> rational people. They didn't want to work any harder than they
> had to. They had to work hard enough as it was.
>
> Craig Smith, modern construction expert

NOWHERE DO THE ANCIENT EGYPTIANS TELL US HOW THEY BUILT THEIR PYR-
amids. Nor, indeed, do they tell us why they built such elaborate tombs.
Over the centuries this lack of knowledge has stimulated the imagination,
leading to the development of many theoretical explanations—some be-
lievable, some definitely less so—of pyramid technology. The best, or most
convincing, of the pyramid theories are those firmly rooted in the archaeological data. However, even among Egyptologists there is still disagree-
ment over some of the fundamental aspects of pyramid construction, and
there is as yet no right or wrong answer to the question, "How were the

pyramids built?" This chapter considers one team's attempt to make sense of the disparate mass of evidence.

A few pyramid theorists have been able to test their ideas by constructing their own small-scale pyramids using modern replicas of ancient tools and techniques. Such experiments can prove very useful, if only to make apparent previously unanticipated problems. Sadly, the experimental work has tended to confirm that pyramid building, mastered by the Egyptians equipped only with the most simple of tools, remains a lost art in our far more mechanized age. The dynastic Egyptians had two advantages that the modern experimenters are unable to reproduce; they had an intimate working knowledge of their own land and its raw materials, and they had access to almost unlimited manpower. Some would add a third advantage: the Egyptians had the enthusiasm, or the religious conviction, to make their dreams come true.

Herodotus tells us exactly how he thinks that the pyramids were built:

> The pyramids were built in steps; some call this technique battlement-wise, or altar-wise. After laying the stones for the base they raised the remaining blocks to their places using machines made of short wooden planks. The first machine elevated them from the ground to the top of the first step. On this there was another machine that received the block and moved it to the second step, where a third machine received the block and moved it still higher. Either they had as many machines as there were steps in the pyramid, or possibly they had a single portable machine which was transferred from layer to layer as the pyramid rose—both accounts are given, and therefore I record both. The upper portion of the pyramid was finished first, then the middle, and finally the part that was lowest and nearest to the ground.
>
> *Histories,* Book 2: 125

However, those who have tried to reproduce this method, using short wooden levers to heave a two-ton block upwards, have not been convinced. The levering technique requires the use of two separate sets of levers, one on each face of the block, plus the use of a support to be slid under the block as each side is raised in turn. This makes the whole process unstable, time-consuming and dangerous, and suggests that levers were probably used only when making final adjustments to blocks that were already in place. Other experimenters have attempted to lift blocks using "machinery" involving counterweights or hydraulic pressure, and have also met with failure. It seems clear that once again Herodotus has been misinformed, and is passing on incorrect information. The Egyptians must have used a more logical, more efficient, safer and possibly simpler method of raising their blocks.

The great Karnak temple of Amen, at Luxor, still bears traces of the ramp and scaffolding associated with a Late Period pylon, or gateway. Here, in order that they might both build and decorate their walls, the workmen had assembled a practical mud-brick and rubble platform alongside each face of the gateway. The platform on the outer face of the gateway could be connected to a long, sloping ramp that allowed the building materials and workers access to the work-face. Space on the other, inner, surface of the gateway was, of course, restricted by the presence of the temple, but here too a shorter, steeper ramp was built and it is this ramp which has partially survived. Usually, building ramps would be dismantled as the project neared completion; it is only because the pylon itself remained un-finished that its ramp was left in place.

Karnak provides our clearest evidence for the use of ramps, but earlier, more fragmentary evidence has also survived: the Middle Kingdom pyra-mid town of Lisht, for example, has traces of a smooth hard stone track-way leading to the pyramid building site. The tradition of ramp use on Egyptian construction sites is therefore firmly established.

At Giza, the roadway connecting the quarry to the pyramid complex is marked by the remains of parallel walls that once enclosed ramps or slides made of limestone chips, gypsum and tafla clay (broken-down shale), which allowed the labourers to drag the blocks upwards, towards the pyra-mid site. Today the area to the south of the pyramids is filled with millions of cubic metres of similar debris. To Mark Lehner, these discarded chips represent the remains of the pyramid ramps, dismantled and dumped back in the quarries as the pyramid was completed. In theory this discovery makes the pyramid building technique clear—the workmen cut blocks of stone, dragged them to the site and then used ramps to raise them to the desired level. This simple explanation, however, leaves too many practical questions unanswered. What form did the ramps take? How exactly were the blocks moved? How long did construction take?

Craig Smith, an American programme manager experienced in the planning of large-scale constructions such as airports and subways, has long been fascinated by the planning of the Great Pyramid. Smith felt that he would be able to apply modern management techniques to one of the most ancient building projects in the world. By first developing a logic diagram (a diagram showing the orderly flow of work) and then creating a critical path schedule (a schedule showing the time needed to complete a construction project consisting of many interrelated tasks) he felt that he might be able to calculate how many workers, for how many years, had been needed to build the pyramid. This theoretical model could then be tested against the more traditional archaeological and historical evidence. In order to compile his schedule, Smith first needed to break down the work into its constituent parts.

Smith started his calculations by considering the evidence preserved in the quarries. As we might expect, the rate of supply of building blocks would have had a direct effect on the rate of pyramid construction. No blocks effectively meant no work: "One of the constraints that one faces is how many blocks can you produce in the quarries and move up to the site with a work crew of a few thousand people, which is what we anticipate would be available for that function."

The Great Pyramid used stone imported from various sources but the bulk of the pyramid, its invisible inner core, was built using inferior limestone cut from a local quarry situated on the Giza Plateau to the south of the pyramid complex. Khaefre and Menkaure were to follow this example; there was no point in moving stone further than was absolutely necessary, and so their quarries were established close to that of Khufu. The quantities of stone extracted from Khufu's principal quarry seem extraordinary today; Mark Lehner has calculated that approximately 2.76 million cubic metres (97.5 million cubic feet) of stone were removed.

The archaeologists have already uncovered the basic implements used by the quarry workers. The industrial complex has yielded evidence of large-scale copper tool production, while in the nearby tombs Zahi Hawass had found both sharp flint blades and substantial hard hammer-stones. In the quarry the marks of the ancient stone-cutters, too, are well preserved, allowing us to reconstruct the cutting of a large soft limestone block with a fair degree of confidence. The masons, having measured and marked out their block, would cut around the sides and then carefully undercut the base using stone tools. Finally, with the roughly shaped block resting precariously on a thin spur of rock plus a large quantity of packing stones, they would use long wooden levers to prise the stone free. Today the Giza quarries show a regular chequered design of raised stone plinths, the uneven bases of the extracted blocks separated by the trenches where the quarrymen squatted to chisel and lever.

For Khufu's pyramid to have been completed within his reign (a minimum of twenty-three years) Mark Lehner has calculated that 322 cubic metres (nearly 11,500 cubic feet) of stone would have had to be cut in the quarry each day—his own experiments have led him to suggest that this would require some 1212 quarry workers at the time of peak stone production. This was hard, tedious, dusty work carried out in the full glare of the sun at maximum possible speed; conditions in the quarry must, at all times, have been very difficult.

Not all the building blocks could be obtained from the Giza Plateau; some stone had to be imported by barge. The fine limestone used in the casing could be found at several sites on the eastern side of the river, with the principal quarry being at Tura. Here the masons were forced to tunnel along the seams of good quality rock, creating galleries in the limestone face. The gypsum used to make mortar came from the Faiyum, while the fifty-six massive slabs of granite used in the burial chamber of the Great Pyramid—estimated to weigh approximately fifty-four tons each—were quarried over 900 kilometres (580 miles) to the south at Aswan. By ancient Egyptian terms this was not an excessive weight. Some of the limestone blocks in the mortuary temple of Menkaure have been estimated to weigh up to two hundred tons; these, however, did not have to be transported by boat.

Granite, far harder than limestone, would have been correspondingly harder to quarry. We know that by the New Kingdom—the time of intensive obelisk production—the surface of the granite was prepared by heating with fire and dousing with water; this cracked the surface of the stone and removed the upper layers of lower quality material. Once the high quality rock had been located and marked out, the sides and underside of the slab were cut by teams of labourers repeatedly knocking hand-held dolomite hammer-stones against the granite surface. Drill holes, occasionally found in Old Kingdom granite monuments, suggest that the masons were also occasionally employing copper drills in conjunction with a sand and water mixture, which would actually cut into the rock. Eventually—and it would have been a very long process—the slab could be freed from the mother-rock, dressed to its final shape and loaded on to a barge. Polishing would come later, at the building site.

It was only the presence of the River Nile which allowed the use of these specific, precious stones throughout the Nile Valley; to transport such vast rocks over hundreds of miles of road or desert would have been impossible. The loading and unloading of a granite slab would, however, have caused huge problems; one mistake and both barge and valuable slab could be lost for ever. Unfortunately the 4th Dynasty builders remain modestly silent about their feats of river transportation and we are forced to turn to classical historian Pliny for a suggestion as to how the barges may have received their heavy cargo:

> A canal was dug from the River Nile to the spot where the obelisk lay and two broad vessels, loaded with blocks of similar stone a foot [30 centimetres] square—the cargo of each amounting to double the size and consequently double the weight of the obelisks—was put beneath it, the extremities of the obelisk remaining supported by the opposite sides of the canal. The blocks of stone were removed and the vessels, being thus gradually lightened, received their burden.
>
> *Natural History,* Book 36: 14

A relief carving in the pyramid causeway of the late 5th Dynasty pharaoh Unas, built some two hundred years after the Great Pyramid, shows a barge carrying two large granite columns from Aswan to Sakkara.

The columns rest end to end, lashed to sleds that in turn appear to lie on wooden scaffolding, which would both help to spread the load on the barge, and assist with its unloading. Seven hundred years later, the New Kingdom Queen Hatchepsut illustrated the moving of her twin obelisks (each estimated to weigh approximately 320 tons) in her mortuary temple at Deir el-Bahari. The obelisks are again shown on the river, lashed to sledges and being towed on a sycamore wood barge by a fleet of twenty-seven smaller boats. Fortunately the flow of the river helps the heavily laden barge on its way.

The Egyptologist Reginald Engelbach suggested that Hatchepsut's barges, brought to the quarry along purpose-built canals, may have been completely surrounded by earth ramps that would allow an obelisk to be raised and manoeuvred into position with relative ease. Once the cargo was loaded and secured to everyone's satisfaction, the barge could then be dug free, the canal being widened if necessary, and towed down the canal and into the river. Unloading could perhaps be achieved by inserting long wooden poles under the supports of the slab and then, as suggested by Pliny, weighting the boat with stones so that it effectively sank below the level of the supporting poles, separating the barge from its cargo. As the Egyptians showed a marked reluctance to change their time-honoured working methods, it seems reasonable to assume that a similar technique may well have been used during the Old Kingdom.

The pyramids, as tombs, had to be built in the Redland, or desert. As they could not be sited on the river bank, the river had to be brought to the pyramid. The Giza Plateau would have been provided with a purpose-built harbour, allowing boats to bring supplies as close as possible to the building site. Stone was the predominant raw material, but copper and wood, too, had to be imported by cargo boat to allow the workmen to perform their duties. The copper, from Sinai, was used to make metal tools in the production area discovered by Mark Lehner, while the wood not only acted as fuel for cooking, brewing, smelting and pottery and mortar production, but was used to make levers, sleds, boats, barges and even packing cases for the transport of delicate statuary. The recycling of the valuable wood—the use of old ship's timbers as levers or trackways, for example—was common practice on Egyptian building sites, while all broken or discarded wooden objects would eventually be used as fuel. This explains why today we find so few wooden objects at dynastic sites. Other resources—food, drink, mud-bricks, clothing—would of course be required to maintain the workforce and have already been considered in Chapter 3.

How, exactly, would the blocks have been moved to the pyramid? Again, we have to look to other sites and other eras to find the answer. In the early Middle Kingdom tomb of Djehutyhotep at Deir el-Bershah, we are shown a colossal statue being moved from the Hatnub alabaster quarry to the river bank. It has been calculated that this statue, some seven metres (twenty-three feet) tall, would have weighed just under sixty tons. The statue itself is bound by ropes on to a wooden sled. This is being dragged by teams of workers over a temporary roadway of wooden planks; the planks are placed in front of the sled and then collected up behind to be repositioned. Rollers are not deemed necessary, and indeed experiments have shown that the use of rollers can actually increase friction and decrease efficiency. However, to help the statue glide and to avoid problems of overheating, water is being used as a lubricant—anyone who has slipped on a wet wooden deck will understand how effective this could be. As the statue was pulled slowly and steadily, its own momentum would help it to glide along.

Experiments conducted by Henri Chevrier in the late 1960s have shown that six men could easily pull a five- to six-ton block using a wooden sled and watered wooden trackway. This would suggest that a pull-ratio of one ton per worker is acceptable; the Djehutyhotep scene, with 172 men pulling a mere sixty tons, or a pull-ratio of 0.3 tons per worker, therefore appears eminently feasible. Indeed, with the pulling of the Djehutyhotep statue it seems that control of the workforce, rather than lack of physical strength, would have been the difficulty. Someone would have needed to ensure that everyone pulled in exactly the same direction, at the same time.

More experiments involving the movement of heavy weights over land have been conducted by European prehistorians seeking to replicate the movement of megaliths to sites such as Stonehenge, Avebury and Carnac; here it has been calculated that 0.5 tons per worker is the standard ratio, but that a gradient makes a great deal of difference—with the slope naturally increasing the slippage. Mark Lehner, on the basis of this and his own experimental work, has calculated that Khufu's pyramid would have employed approximately 1360 stone hauliers to move 340 blocks each day.

While the Egyptians regularly used donkeys to transport loads by road, cattle were the draught animals employed on building sites. Here they would either work alongside, or instead of, men. The Middle Kingdom complex of Mentuhotep at Deir el-Bahari has even yielded cattle bones—presumably oxen rather than cows—on the building site. Given the presence of an unexpectedly large number of cattle bones at Mark Lehner's production site, this opens up the intriguing—although perhaps somewhat unrealistic—prospect of the Giza construction workers first working alongside their cattle, and then eating them. Whatever hauling method was used, however, the provision of a firm artificial trackway made of wood, mud-brick or stone chip was essential. As many experimental archaeologists have found, simply dragging the block across the desert would cause it to halt and sink in the sand. Nile mud was in relatively short supply at Giza and so, as we have already seen, the roadway to the quarry was made of tons of hard stone chips and tafla clay, quarried locally.

By the time the limestone core blocks started to arrive on site, the bedrock would have been prepared, the base platform of Tura limestone would have been levelled and measured out and the orientation of the pyramid would have been determined. Unfortunately this preliminary work, carried out using the most simple of survey tools (plumb-bobs, measuring ropes and rods, and wooden set-squares and square levels), leaves little trace in the archaeological record. Conscientious builders, of course, deliberately clean up their sites as they leave so that it is only within the damaged structure of Menkaure's pyramid that we are able to see the painted red lines used as reference points.

We know that the Egyptians had developed their mathematical and their measuring skills alongside their writing; even the archaic Narmer Palette shows an awareness of the canon of proportions, the system used for measuring in art. Now the architects were able to measure out the pyramid using a method shown in the New Kingdom foundation ritual known as the "stretching of the cord," when symbolic measurements were taken using string extended between wooden pegs. This could be combined with a mathematical formula, known since the 1st Dynasty, for measuring the inclination of the pyramid face. Without using our system of degrees, the Egyptian *seked* expressed angles as a ratio of the horizontal to the vertical measurement.

Nowhere do the pyramid builders tell us how they aligned their monuments. We are therefore forced to fall back on informed speculation when discussing the precise orientation of the Great Pyramid. This suggests a detailed understanding of astronomy and of geometry, allowing the pyramid to be aligned by reference to the stars, in particular the North Star or Pole Star. The Egyptians were to develop a centuries-long interest in the night sky and the extent of their astronomical knowledge is made obvious by the astronomical ceilings found in the New Kingdom tombs of Senenmut and Seti I. Speculation that the pyramid might instead have been oriented solely by the sun—perhaps by measuring shadow—seems unlikely, as this would have been a less accurate method. However, there would of course be no reason why the architects could not combine the two techniques.

It appears that, having established their north–south line, the pyramid site was surrounded by a series of temporary reference posts strung together; each block could then be properly aligned before setting. The fact that the top of the Great Pyramid has a slight twist confirms the difficulties experienced when dealing with the uppermost levels which would, by their very nature, have allowed the masons a restricted working space. It is generally assumed that the topmost blocks would have been levered into place by workmen standing on wooden scaffolding.

The once popular theory that the base of the pyramid may have been levelled using water now seems unlikely as such an operation would involve vast quantities of water being carried to the site. Levelling using water eventually appeared on the Egyptian building site in the Roman era. Instead, it seems that the square level, a simple wooden device incorporating a plumb-bob suspended from an A-frame that allowed the surveyor to read a level, was used. Eventually the base of the pyramid was to show a deviation of just 2.1 centimetres (slightly less than one inch).

Just as the rate of cutting and delivery of the blocks would have a controlling or limiting effect on the speed of pyramid growth, so would the rate at which the masons and stone-cutters could lay and dress the blocks.

While hard stone would be dressed in the quarry, where there were suitable experts on hand, the softer limestone blocks would be cut to their final shape at the pyramid face. Not all the blocks would need to be dressed—those destined to form the core could be left alone—but those that were to form part of a flat wall had to be smoothed before they came into contact with their neighbouring blocks. Egyptologist Rainer Stadelman has calculated that to complete their work the masons must have been able to lay approximately 340 blocks per day, working at the most a ten-hour day for at least nineteen years. This means that a limestone block would have to be cut, delivered to the site and set in place at the phenomenal rate of one block every two minutes! At the pyramid face, Lehner estimates that it would require ten men one hour to set each block; as the blocks were arriving at an approximate rate of thirty-four per hour, this would imply a workforce of 340 men, working at maximum speed.

While most experts would now agree that the blocks were raised up the pyramid by a system of ramps, there has been much scholarly argument over the precise ramp design. Archaeology is of little help here; the Great Pyramid shows no trace of its original ramp(s) while other pyramids, which do provide evidence of ramps, show that there was no universal system. It seems that Egypt's builders suited their ramps to the local conditions of each pyramid.

Over the years, theorists have suggested several possible models for the building of Khufu's pyramid; the ramp, or ramps, could, for example, have been internal or external. It may have been on one side, all four sides, or on the corners. It/they might have wrapped itself/themselves around the pyramid, or could have zig-zagged up one side, although both these methods have the considerable disadvantage of introducing bends that would have been difficult to negotiate with the heavy blocks. A more serious objection to the wrap-around model is that the ramp itself tends to obscure the shape of the pyramid and might encourage misalignment of the slope. The one ramp that most experts agree seems impossible is the single, simple ramp reaching to the very summit of the pyramid; such a ramp would need to be lengthened as the pyramid rose, and would eventually take up more material, and involve more work, than the construction of the pyramid itself.

Craig Smith felt it reasonable to assume that the Egyptians, eminently rational people, would not embark on more work than they absolutely had to. Using three-dimensional computer graphics to test his theories, he concluded that the most efficient method would have been to build a substantial, straight ramp up to a third of the height of the pyramid. This would allow the placement of half or more of the blocks. Then a smaller ramp would be wrapped around the pyramid, allowing the placement of the upper blocks, which would be both fewer in number and smaller in size. This upper ramp would have to be attached to the pyramid itself by limestone supports, which could then be removed as the ramp itself was dismantled, working from the summit downwards. At the same time the outer casing of Tura limestone would be added, again working from the top downwards.

While there is no proof that this model is the correct one, the archaeological evidence, in the form of undressed casing stones recovered by Zahi Hawass at the base of the queens' pyramids, suggests that the Great Pyramid may indeed have been fitted with protrusions. These would have allowed the suspension of a wrap-around style ramp starting either at ground level or part-way up the pyramid face.

Having considered the individual complex techniques of pyramid construction, Smith was able to draw up a detailed management plan involving every aspect of the project. This indicated that the pyramid could possibly have been built in just ten years, using the following schedule:

> Preparation of site: 2–3 years
> Construction: 5 years
> Removing ramps, cleaning, etc.: 2 years

The peak workforce, following this schedule, would have been required in years four, five and six, with as many as 40,000 labourers being required on site as the blocks were hauled up the ramps and on to the pyramid. As the pyramid rose in height fewer blocks would be needed, and fewer workers could actually work on the pyramid itself and so this number would gradually tail off.

Smith's total, although considerably less than that suggested by Herodotus, is almost double that calculated by the Egyptologists Lehner and Hawass on the basis of the archaeological evidence uncovered in the Pyramid City. Lehner, having made his own estimates of the workforce based on his own practical experience, has suggested a total of approximately 4000 primary labourers (approximately 1212 quarry workers, 1360 hauliers and 360 masons) plus those engaged in building ramps, making tools, preparing food and so on. His estimated total workforce is therefore in the region of twenty to twenty-five thousand.

However, Smith was expecting his workforce to build their pyramid in the minimum possible time of ten years. The archaeologists, knowing that Khufu died after at least twenty-three years on the throne with his pyramid not quite complete, and being fairly confident that the king would have started to build his pyramid as soon as he came to the throne, have suggested that the workmen may have toiled for twenty years or more rather than ten. By doubling the time taken to work on the project, it is possible to substantially reduce the number of workers required at any given time. Half of forty thousand, a reasonable reduction, would tie in very well with the five thousand permanent workers (those employed to provision the Pyramid City, plus those employed as élite artisans) and up to fifteen thousand temporary workers postulated by Mark Lehner and Zahi Hawass.

CHAPTER FIVE

Why?
The Unity
of the Pyramids

> I am almost more interested now in how the pyramids built
> Egypt than how the Egyptians built the pyramids.
>
> Mark Lehner

HERODOTUS' ACCOUNT OF TENS OF THOUSANDS OF SLAVES TOILING TO BUILD
the Great Pyramid is now firmly relegated to the realms of fiction. But who
were the anonymous workers who arrived in such vast numbers to work
on the pyramid site? The skeletons themselves hold vital clues to their origins. At Cairo University Medical School Moamina Kamal has embarked
on a programme to compare DNA taken from the 4500-year-old workers'
bones to DNA taken from modern Egyptians. This work is still in progress,
but the preliminary, unpublished results are highly suggestive.

First, dispelling the myth that the ancient Egyptians would have been
incapable of designing and constructing such sophisticated monuments,

the DNA studies indicate that the pyramid builders were the forebears of the modern Egyptians. This confirmation of the "Egyptian-ness" of the pyramids, something that Egyptologists have never doubted, is nevertheless a welcome antidote to the more bizarre theories that have surfaced over the years. Zahi Hawass, unsurprised but pleased by the results, has noted that: "It is very important to know that they were Egyptians. They were not people who came from out of space. They were not aliens. They were not from lost civilizations. . . ."

Secondly, as Dr Kamal explains: "From our preliminary studies we can see people coming from the whole Nile Valley, from Aswan to the Nile Delta, and so I can say that all the Nile Valley citizens at that time were participating in the building of the pyramids."

This evidence of people travelling the length of the country to work on the pyramids is interesting, suggesting as it does two different models of pyramid construction: the traditional, or compulsory *corvée* model, and the newer, volunteer labour model. We will consider these models in turn.

The first model, founded on the supposition that no one would volunteer to work on the pyramid site, suggests that people were compelled to work on the project, with the provincial governors expected to provide a given number of labourers each year. The Egyptians, although they had no need of a state-wide system of artificial irrigation, were occasionally forced to embark on large-scale civic projects such as the cutting of canals or the strengthening of boundary walls. In addition, pharaoh occasionally felt the need to confirm his status by building a splendid monument—usually a temple—which would serve as a permanent testament to his piety and power. Pyramids fall into this second class of prestige rather than necessary projects. All these major construction projects required the services of skilled craftsmen—architects, surveyors, scribes and so on—plus a massive amount of man/woman power.

There is good evidence, dating back to the Old Kingdom, to show that these projects were masterminded by professional government employees but were actually carried out by workers conscripted from the local communities under the system of *corvée*, or temporary forced labour. *Corvée*, in the absence of money, was a form of state taxation. Labourers were summoned by local officials acting under the orders of the vizier's office. They were taken from home, accommodated in barracks or workhouses—there was one such workhouse attached to the Great Prison of Thebes—and fed and clothed until they had completed their community service and were free to return home.

While the wider community benefited from this system, the individual workers received no compensation for their labours. Naturally the *corvée* call-up was dreaded. A few lucky Egyptians were exempted by statute. Others were able to "persuade" the administrators to overlook them by administering a suitable bribe, so that it was generally the poorer members of society who were in any real danger of being taken away to work. Once enlisted, escape was not advised. A 12th Dynasty document, today known as the Brooklyn Papyrus, lists some seventy-five men and one woman who were foolish enough to run away without completing their work. The courts, taking a dim view of such anti-social behaviour, were empowered to seize the families of the deserters as hostages against their return. Once the deserters had surrendered, or had been caught, the families were in all but one case released, while the offender was left to face the consequence of his or her actions.

It is clear from the Brooklyn Papyrus that women as well as men were summoned to *corvée* labour, although we are not told what type of work they were expected to perform. It may be that the work was divided by sex. It also seems obvious that the *corvée* workers were taken as individuals, not as family units. Could we then expect to find women labourers, as opposed to the wives who accompanied the élite artisans, among the temporary pyramid workers? On the basis of this evidence, possibly, although we may deduce that single women only would be taken. Given the traditional respect for the role of wife and mother, it seems highly unlikely that wives would be forced away from their husbands and children. And, as dynastic women tended to marry and produce children in their early teens, this would have automatically excluded many. Indeed, given that the temporary workers were being summoned to perform intensive physical labour, it seems highly likely that men would have been selected in preference to women, at least for the primary pyramid building work. We have only indirect evidence that women may have worked on Egypt's construction sites and, although this need not rule out the possibility of women being summoned to work in the pyramid city, it does suggest that the temporary workforce is likely to have been substantially, if not entirely, male.

An alternative model has been put forward by Mark Lehner and Zahi Hawass, who sums it up: "The Great Pyramid was the national project of the whole nation." Lehner has compared the building of the pyramids to North American Amish barn-raisings. Here, the entire community gathers together to achieve a common goal, with work being allocated along traditional lines between men and women, the old and the young. Individual members of the community may have little wish to participate, but social and family pressure ensures that they do. From this, Lehner has gone on to suggest that the pyramid builders may have been volunteers, gathered together out of a sense of civic duty and social rather than state compulsion. Barn-raisings, and perhaps pyramid buildings, thus became social as well as economic events. A second parallel may perhaps be suggested with the system of kibbutzim in Israel where volunteers, often the western young in search of adventure, are persuaded to donate their labour for a common good and the promise of a good time.

The young of Old Kingdom Egypt, leaving their villages of a few hundred inhabitants to stay at the pyramid city of fifteen thousand like-minded individuals dedicated to the same project, may well have seen pyramid building as a glorious experience. Certainly Zahi Hawass, having discovered miniature mud-brick pyramids among the tombs of the Giza workers, believes that the symbolism of the pyramid was already strong enough to encourage people, both men and women, to offer their labour. If the pyramid was indeed built by volunteers, and assuming that this was not an all-male bonding experience, we may perhaps expect to find more women among the workforce as entire families may have travelled together to work at Giza. This theory can to a certain extent be supported by the evidence from the on-going excavations at the workers' cemetery where females, interred as part of family groups rather than as individuals, make up approximately 50 percent of the burials.

For the moment we must leave the question of the assembly of the workforce—compulsory versus volunteer—unanswered for lack of evidence. One thing, however, is very obvious. Whatever the mechanism for assembling the workforce, it was a highly efficient one. There was little advance in building technology between the 2nd and 4th Dynasties. What then allowed Djoser, Snefru, Khufu and Khaefre to abandon mud-brick architecture and embark on such ambitious projects? Mark Lehner is certain of the answer: "The advances were not in tools, techniques and technology; the advances were in social organization."

The building of the Great Pyramid was an undeniable triumph of organization with first-class planning and coordination on a scale that would be impressive even today. This coordination extended far beyond the Giza Plateau, so that up and down the Nile Valley and across the Delta there were farmers, miners, sailors, quarrymen and of course labourers closely involved in a single national project. Almost all of the adult working population, either directly or indirectly, must have worked to build the pyramid. The surplus resources from the provinces flowed to Giza, making everyone aware of pharaoh's right and ability to control Egypt's wealth. Without unrestricted access to his country's resources, Khufu could never have built his pyramid.

Pyramid building forced the development of a sophisticated bureaucratic system that could cope with the demands of maybe twenty thousand workers. The two hallmarks of the Egyptian organizational approach—the appointment of officials whose particular responsibilities are reflected in their titles, and the splitting of large numbers of labourers into efficient working units—is very much apparent in the Giza workers' cemetery. When faced with a seemingly impossible task—the construction of a vast monument—the Egyptian response was to break the work down into a series of small, manageable tasks, with each individual task under the control of a professional manager. It can be no coincidence that, at the time that the pyramids were being built, we see the first signs of a professional civil service starting to emerge in Egypt. While the king and the immediate royal family were able to retain their semi-divine role, they were now supported by ministers chosen by ability, not birth.

In the introduction to this book we sought an explanation of the unifying force that helped to weld the disparate city-states of pre-unification Egypt into one land. It may well be that in pyramid building—in dedicating the labour and resources of the masses to one glorious purpose—the Old Kingdom pharaohs had found a mechanism that would reinforce the unity of their newly created land.

Part Three

▲ ▲ ▲ ▲ ▲ ▲ ▲

On the Trail of Tutankhamen

On the Trail
of Tutankhamen

The decisive moment had arrived. With trembling hands I made
a tiny breach in the upper left-hand corner. . . . At first I could see
nothing, the hot air escaping from the chamber causing the candle flame to flicker, but presently, as my eyes grew accustomed
to the light, details of the room within emerged slowly from the
mist, strange animals, statues, and gold—everywhere the glint of
gold. For the moment—an eternity it must have seemed to the
others standing by—I was struck dumb with amazement, and
when Lord Carnarvon, unable to stand the suspense any longer,
enquired anxiously, "Can you see anything?" it was all I could do
to get out the words, "Yes, wonderful things."

Howard Carter

IN 1922 BRITAIN WAS PROFOUNDLY DEPRESSED, SUFFERING THE AFTER EF-
fects of years of bloody war followed by a devastating outbreak of in-

fluenza. Howard Carter's spectacular discovery of Tutankhamen's burial in the Valley of the Kings was just what was needed to lift the nation's spirits. As Carter embarked on his lifelong mission to record and clear tomb KV 62, scores of journalists rushed to Luxor. Soon Tutankhamen was a household name—indeed, enterprising lawyers in America tried to patent it—as "Egyptomania" swept fashionable society.

Ancient Egypt had been fashionable before. In 1798 Napoleon's Egyptian campaign had inspired a generation of interior designers and had led to the development of the Egyptian Hall, an extremely popular amusement palace in Piccadilly. Here Londoners were to be entertained by the master showman Belzoni unrolling both a human and a monkey mummy. In 1817, as Percy Bysshe Shelley penned his Egypt-inspired sonnet "Ozymandias," the British Museum was drawing the crowds with a display that included the newly arrived "Younger Memnon," a colossal head of Ramesses II. This earlier interest in Egypt, however, was through necessity very much object-based. Hieroglyphs had not yet been decoded, the names of the pharaohs went unread and dead Egyptians were treated as curiosities, not real people. A century later, as Carter revealed his find to the world, it was not only possible to name the dead king but to place Tutankhamen in his correct dynastic setting.

To a general public mourning the loss of a generation of young men, the discovery of Tutankhamen's tomb created a new romantic hero: a young king, undeniably rich and almost certainly handsome, lost for centuries in a gold-packed grave. The untimely death of Lord Carnarvon, which came soon after the discovery of his tomb, added a pleasing touch of supernatural horror to the story of riches and royalty. No publicist could have dreamed up a better plot.

Egyptologists regarded the discovery with more restraint. Tutankhamen emerged from his coffins confirmed as one of the last monarchs of Egypt's mighty 18th Dynasty, the final king of the great Tuthmoside family and a relatively minor figure in Egypt's long history. His tomb, so generously equipped with golden artefacts designed to amuse a young man for all eternity, was if anything rather a disappointment. With virtually no written material, it seemed to offer little chance of explaining the muddled complexities of Tuthmoside family life. Who exactly was Tutankhamen?

Who were his parents, his siblings and his children? And what happened to end his dynastic line? The king himself is stubbornly silent on these matters. As Howard Carter boxed up his golden treasures and sent them off to Cairo he must have believed that, contrary to public opinion, he had made little contribution to the understanding of Egyptian history.

Today, with advances in medical techniques that would have astounded Carter and his contemporaries, the importance of the discoveries in the Valley of the Kings is undergoing a rapid reassessment. Cairo Museum is home to many royal mummies, including most of the 18th Dynasty monarchs. These bodies, together with the well-provenanced remains recovered from Tutankhamen's tomb, offer scientists the chance of exploring the genetic make-up of the Tuthmoside kings. The information so obtained may be used to prove, or even disprove, history derived from more conventional written and archaeological sources.

While this work is still in its preliminary stages, its potential is amazing. Family relationships, incestuous marriages and inherited diseases—the personal details of 18th Dynasty life for so long lost in the mists of time—may now be revealed in the science lab. In the words of microbiologist Dr Scott Woodward: "We now have the beginnings of some DNA evidence from the 18th Dynasty. Combined with all of the historical information that has come to light in the past hundred years and all of the other reconstructions of what went on in the 18th Dynasty I think the DNA adds a whole new perspective, a whole new angle to being able to understand who these people were, how they were related to each other and how they interacted."

CHAPTER SIX

When?
The Tangled History
of the 18th Dynasty

The 18th Dynasty is, I think, without question the most famous
of the dynasties of ancient Egypt. It represents the period of
time when Egypt was imperial, and conquered much of the
Middle East. The most famous (for most people at least) of the
pharaohs lived in the 18th Dynasty. And, even though it is the
best documented of the dynasties, it still has some of the most
unanswered questions. . . .

Wilfred Griggs, archaeologist

OVER FIFTEEN HUNDRED YEARS HAD PASSED SINCE THE LEGENDARY MENES
marched northwards to unite his country. Now, as the 17th Dynasty drew
to a close, history was poised to repeat itself as a Theban ruler embarked
on a campaign to reunite his troubled land.

Ahmose was a member of a dynamic and highly ambitious military family. His grandfather, father and brother had each fought to dislodge the Hyksos kings who ruled northern Egypt, with both his father, Sekenenre Tao II "The Brave," and his brother, Kamose, dying in pursuit of their dream of unity. His grandmother, Tetisheri, and his mother, Ahhotep I, were strong, politically active figures and the widowed Ahhotep, "one who has accomplished the rites and taken care of Egypt," had proved a worthy regent for her infant son.

Ahmose, inheriting his throne at maybe five years of age, had been forced to bide his time. Now his fight with the Hyksos was to be no sudden glorious triumph, but a hard war of attrition as the hated foreigners were slowly but surely pushed back into the Delta. By the end of Year 16 of his reign the Hyksos had gone, chased out of Egypt and eastwards into Palestine. Ahmose was now the acknowledged pharaoh of all Egypt and future generations would, in recognition of his great feat and despite the fact that his father and brothers were considered to belong to the 17th Dynasty, regard him as both the first king of the 18th Dynasty and the founder of the New Kingdom. Egyptian dynasties were never constructed along strict family lines.

Ahmose-Nefertari, sister–wife to Ahmose, proved to be another high-profile queen, the first to be accorded the title of "God's Wife of Amen," an honour financed by a substantial independent estate. Already we can see that Theban queen consorts were very different to their invisible, insignificant Old and Middle Kingdom predecessors. The New Kingdom queen has become a personality; she is recognized as a vital component of her husband's reign—for it seems that no king would be complete without a queen—and bears a range of titles and intricate crowns that reflect her increasingly important political and religious role. From now onwards, when we consider the royal family, we will be considering the women as well as the men.

Ahmose-Nefertari outlived her husband to serve as regent for her young son, Amenhotep. Amenhotep I was to rule for twenty-one conventional years, his reign seeing continued southerly expansion into Nubia. In death both Amenhotep I and Ahmose-Nefertari were to be worshipped at the newly established workmen's village of Deir el-Medina, where their cults lasted for many centuries.

Here the direct family line of Ahmose, a line that had cut across the artificial 17th–18th Dynasty divide, ended. Amenhotep and his sister-consort Meritamen had no living son and so, rather than look to the children born in the royal harem, Amenhotep turned to the army to find a worthy successor. General Tuthmosis, son of the lady Senisonb, possibly a descendant of a collateral branch of the family, became Tuthmosis I, his wife Queen Ahmose. The Tuthmoside era had begun.

Tuthmosis and his descendants were to become increasingly wealthy monarchs with access to almost unlimited resources, which would allow them to build in stone on a scale not seen since the pyramid age. Now, however, the preferred royal monuments would be highly visible temples, obelisks and colossal statues rather than imposing tombs. The reunification of Egypt, and the successful reimposition of central control under a professional civil service, had led to a spectacular economic boom. As international trade flourished, and as Egypt's sphere of influence widened, the royal treasury—or rather the many royal warehouses, for this was still a moneyless society where all dues were paid in labour or in kind—was filled to bursting point with taxes and tribute received from a growing number of client states. Already, as Tuthmosis ascended to his throne, Egypt was the richest and most powerful state in the ancient world.

Egypt's wealth needed to be guarded. Ahmose had set the military standard for subsequent 18th Dynasty pharaohs, most of whom would be eager to emphasize their role as warrior kings able to defend their land and gods against all enemies. Hitherto Egypt's rulers had rarely needed to prove their prowess in battle. Few within Egypt had dared to challenge the position of their semi-divine king, while her geographical and cultural isolation, her lack of immediate neighbours, had so protected Egypt from the dangers of foreign invasion that there had been no perceived need to establish a standing army. Now the situation had changed and pharaoh's growing involvement in international affairs meant that he could no longer afford to ignore events outside his borders.

The late Bronze Age was a time of increasing movement—trade, diplomacy, migration and military activity—throughout the entire Near East, and Egypt needed to prove that she could not be intimidated. The image of Narmer smiting his enemy was now picked up and magnified, so that large-scale scenes of pharaoh defending his country became a standard decoration for temple walls. Tuthmosis used his experience as a soldier to develop the New Kingdom army into an efficient fighting machine that could be used both to protect Egypt's interests and expand her territories.

Ahmose and Tuthmosis, as Thebans, revered their local god Amen, "The Hidden One." Credited with inspiring the victory against the Hyksos, Amen's fortunes had become inextricably linked to those of the royal family. As pharaoh became richer and more powerful so did Amen, until eventually he took his rightful role as the most influential god, and one of the major landowners, of the Egyptian Empire. The Karnak temple, Amen's principal home, grew outwards and upwards as successive kings donated increasingly elaborate stone extensions that dominated the earlier mud-brick chapels.

Meanwhile the more ancient, northern solar cult of Re suffered from the dwindling royal interest. Thebes was now the acknowledged religious capital of Egypt, with the royal necropolis sited on the west bank, opposite the Karnak temple. The new pharaohs, while recognizing the importance of both the traditional capital, Memphis, and the new capital, Thebes, were reluctant to commit themselves to any particular city, preferring instead a more mobile approach to government. The Tuthmoside royal court had no permanent base but travelled slowly up and down the Nile, staying in a series of short-term rest houses, the "Mooring Places of Pharaoh," dotted at strategic points along the river. Thus pharaoh became obvious to all his people.

Tuthmosis I, a highly experienced general, was all too well aware that a change of ruling family might be misinterpreted as a time of weakness. He therefore determined to establish his authority from the outset. In Year 2 Egyptian troops marched southwards, advancing past the Third Cataract and returning home leaving a chastened Nubia firmly under Egyptian control. Next pharaoh turned his attention to his eastern neighbours. Ahmose, in expelling the Hyksos, had established a protective buffer-zone in Palestine. Now Tuthmosis was to take things much further. The Egyptian army advanced eastwards from Memphis, crossing the River Euphrates and entering lands ruled by the ancient kingdom of Mitanni. Having set a victorious stela on the bank of the Euphrates, and successfully demonstrated

Egypt's military might to all, Tuthmosis travelled home, pausing only for a satisfyingly dangerous elephant hunt in Syria.

Back home, a major building programme was under way with the Karnak temple benefiting from an impressive series of improvements. Opposite the temple, on the west bank of the Nile, the royal architect Ineni was busy excavating the king's rock-cut tomb. This was to follow the new custom, established as much through geographical necessity as through theological belief, of separating the burial chamber from the mortuary temple. As we have already seen, the pyramid kings built their mortuary temples beside their pyramids so that offerings could be made close to the body of the deceased. In the Giza desert, where there was plenty of room, this did not cause a problem. Now, however, the narrow, cliff-bound geography of the Theban necropolis was less obliging. It would be impossible to build either pyramids or mortuary temples in the steep Valley of the Kings, and irresponsible to dig burial chambers on the flood-prone desert fringes.

The obvious answer was to abandon the pyramid form, a form primarily associated with the sun god Re, while separating the burial chamber from its temple. This solution—theologically acceptable, as Amen was now the dominant deity—offered the welcome prospect of hiding the entrance to the burial chamber from the necropolis thieves; now there was a real chance that the burials of the kings could lie safe, for ever. Those who regretted the passing of the pyramid were comforted by the presence of the Theban mountain whose triangular shape now offered a gigantic natural pyramid protecting all the royal burials.

The newly independent mortuary temples were, as the pyramid complexes before them, funded by generous royal endowments of land and assets. The temples were therefore able to function as self-administered economic centres complete with all the offices, storerooms and granaries needed to receive, store and redistribute the produce or "offerings" sent from the estates. This was storage on a very large scale indeed: Egyptologist Barry Kemp has calculated that the 19th Dynasty Ramesseum, mortuary temple of Ramesses II, could, if filled, have housed enough grain to feed approximately thirty-four hundred families. The boats, loaded with grain, which sailed up the canals to the temple warehouses, were providing rations that could be used to pay the temple employees and which the king might, in times of shortage, use to pay his own workers.

Egypt's increasing literacy—her monumental inscriptions, tomb and temple walls and papyri—provide us with a more detailed historical framework than was available in our study of the Old Kingdom. We know that Tuthmosis, middle-aged at his accession, reigned for no more than fifteen years. As Queen Ahmose had no living son he left his throne to Tuthmosis, his son by Mutnofret, a high-born lady of uncertain origin. In order to consolidate the younger Tuthmosis' right to rule he was married to his half-sister, Hatchepsut, daughter of Tuthmosis I and Ahmose.

Tuthmosis II also set out to be a conventional New Kingdom monarch, slightly handicapped by a shortage of enemies willing to allow him to prove himself a successful warrior king. No one would put up a serious challenge to Egypt's might, and honour was eventually satisfied by a short Nubian campaign and an expedition to reinforce Egypt's control of Palestine. Meanwhile building works continued at Karnak, and the country prospered. Queen Hatchepsut bore her brother one daughter, Neferure, but no son, and the untimely death of Tuthmosis II saw the throne pass to Tuthmosis III, the infant son of Tuthmosis II and a shadowy lady of the harem, Isis. As the new king was a minor, Queen Hatchepsut was called upon to act as his guardian.

For two years the queen acted as a blameless regent, allowing the young king to take precedence on all formal occasions. By the end of Year 7, however, Hatchepsut had herself become king of Egypt, co-ruler and indeed dominant partner to Tuthmosis III. Quite what brought about this astonishing development we shall probably never know, but the situation seems to have been acceptable to all concerned, and history has preserved no record of anyone attempting to dislodge the new king from her position of power. Hatchepsut herself justified her rule by emphasizing her position as the daughter of Amen. The story of her divine conception and birth was to be told in the most literal of terms on the wall of her mortuary temple at Deir el-Bahari: "She smiled at his majesty [the god Amen]. He went to her, his penis erect. He gave his heart to her. . . . She was filled with joy at the sight of his beauty. His love passed into her limbs. The palace was flooded with the god's fragrance, and all his perfumes were as from Punt."

Here we see Hatchepsut being created in the form of a male child, and here we see the right of the female pharaoh to rule being acknowledged by Amen himself.

For hundreds of years pharaoh had been depicted as a vigorous, confident and physically perfect male. There had been variations on this theme—we have already seen that the Old Kingdom pharaohs were lofty, awe-inspiring individuals while the Middle Kingdom monarchs chose to reveal a more human aspect to their regality—but these were very minor differences. Egypt's artists and sculptors knew what a king should look like, and they now started to depict their new monarch in the time-honoured poses and garments. Hatchepsut was depicted with a male breastless body, dressed in the royal regalia of short kilt, crown or head-cloth, broad collar and false beard. To the uninitiated, Egypt's new pharaoh was a man.

This is confirmation, if ever we needed it, of the complexities and pitfalls of Egyptian art. Hatchepsut was not intending to fool anyone into thinking that she was male—her inscriptions made her gender obvious to all who could read—but she did want to demonstrate that she could be a true king in the time-honoured mould. She knew that a king was essential for the maintenance of *maat*, or the status quo; without *maat*, Egypt would quickly be reduced to the dreaded state of chaos. Hatchepsut's statues, accessible to all in our museums and galleries, were not portraits designed for close public inspection; they were temple furniture, to be seen almost exclusively by the gods who needed to be convinced that Egypt had an effective king.

Hatchepsut embarked upon an ambitious building programme that encompassed not only the erection of new monuments but also the conservation of some dilapidated old ones; by restoring the monuments of her predecessors, Hatchepsut was again demonstrating her ability to maintain *maat* and her fitness to rule. Thebes benefited from extensions to the Karnak temple and from the erection of the west bank Deir el-Bahari mortuary temple, a monument classed by many as one of the most beautiful buildings of the ancient world. Hatchepsut's foreign policy followed strictly conventional lines. Egypt's borders would be maintained if not expanded, while international trade flourished—with one spectacularly successful mission to the faraway land of Punt being recorded on the Deir el-Bahari temple walls.

After more than twenty years Hatchepsut relaxed her hold on the throne allowing Tuthmosis III, now a fully grown man, to play a more prominent role in matters of state. Tuthmosis, commander-in-chief of the army, assumed the awesome responsibility of defending Egypt's borders. Egypt was being troubled by sporadic unrest among her eastern client states, and Tuthmosis found himself forced to commit his troops to the first of the series of military campaigns needed to reimpose firm control on both the Levant and Nubia.

Hatchepsut died after twenty-two years on the throne, leaving Tuthmosis to rule alone for a further thirty-three years. Much of his solo reign would be spent abroad, fighting to consolidate Egypt's international position. In Year 33 Tuthmosis was able to emulate his grandfather by crossing the Euphrates and then returning to Egypt via a Syrian elephant hunt. By Year 42 the boundaries of the empire were at last secure and Tuthmosis was able to relax. He now looked inwards, towards the improvement of his own land. Once again Karnak echoed to the masons' hammers, while all the major Egyptian towns benefited from his attentions. In Year 51 Tuthmosis appointed his son as co-regent, and two years later it was Amenhotep II who buried Egypt's greatest warrior king in the Valley of the Kings.

Tuthmosis III, long-lived warrior and builder, proved a hard act to follow. His immediate successors, competent monarchs both, remain very much in his shade. Amenhotep II, a famous athlete, both built within Egypt and instigated successful military campaigns. After twenty-three years he was succeeded by his younger son, Tuthmosis IV who, as a prince, had become perhaps the world's first "rescue" archaeologist by clearing away the sand that now covered the sphinx at Giza. Tuthmosis reigned for a mere nine years, during which time he was able to suppress a Nubian rebellion and raise an obelisk at the Karnak temple. His untimely death left the teenage Amenhotep III as king and the dowager queen Mutemwia as regent.

Amenhotep, abandoning the tradition of brother–sister or brother–half-sister marriages that had so far characterized his dynasty, chose as his consort the commoner Tiy, daughter of the official Yuya and his wife Thuyu.

Tiy, far from being handicapped by her more humble origins, was to pick up and develop the tradition of the influential queen-consort that had lapsed somewhat in the post-Hatchepsut era.

By now the 18th Dynasty was some two centuries old, fabulously wealthy and so well organized that the country seemed to run itself with effortless ease. The civil service, the priesthood and the army functioned as efficient, independent units with their own structures of command, each ultimately falling under the control of the king. The new king was unable to prove his prowess on the battlefield—foreigners wanted to be his friend, not his enemy—and so he exhibited bravery on the hunting field until a very minor Nubian campaign allowed him to claim his rightful place as a mighty warrior king.

Amenhotep, relieved of the need to fund extravagant military campaigns, put his resources to good use, building at all the principal Egyptian sites and investing in a vast number of colossal images of himself. Ramesses II, a great admirer of Amenhotep III, was later to usurp many of these statues, converting them into his own image so that Amenhotep is now seriously under-represented in the record of Egyptian art. In the newly fashioned sandstone Luxor temple, a temple dedicated to the celebration of the divine royal soul, Amenhotep reintroduced the legend of divine birth by copying Hatchepsut's story almost word for word. He used the story not, as the more insecure Hatchepsut had done, as a way of justifying his own rule but as a means of confirming his own status.

His own divinity was starting to fascinate the king. Theology, and centuries of tradition, dictated that the semi-divine pharaoh would became fully divine only at death. Already, however, the living Amenhotep was starting to hint at greater things. He was recognized as the embodiment of the god Ptah and worshipped as such in the temples of Memphis, while in the provinces, away from the traditional cult-centres, things had gone a step further: Amenhotep's Nubian Soleb temple celebrated the king as the local god Nebmaatre (or Amenhotep III) Lord of Nubia. Without ever neglecting Amen, Amenhotep started to diversify his religious interests. In particular, he developed an interest in solar theology, focusing on one god, the Aten, an obscure form of the sun-god Re and symbol of divine kingship. Now Amenhotep was able to exploit the Aten cult as a means of developing his own latent divinity, a divinity that was to be made increasingly apparent after the celebration of his *heb sed*, or thirty-year jubilee.

Eventually, after thirty-eight years on the throne, and suffering from terrible toothache, Amenhotep III died. Crown Prince Tuthmosis was already dead and so Amenhotep was succeeded by his younger son, the hitherto invisible Amenhotep IV. The fact that we have not seen Prince Amenhotep before is not unusual—royal children, boys in particular, were seldom accorded any publicity. Now, like his father before him, the new king chose a non-royal wife. Nefertiti's parentage is nowhere made clear. However, strong circumstantial evidence suggests that she was the daughter of the courtier Ay, who was most probably a son of Yuya and Thuyu and therefore the brother of Tiy and the cousin of Amenhotep IV.

The commoner queen was able to overcome her relatively humble beginnings and follow the precedent set by her mother-in-law, Tiy, to become perhaps the most influential queen-consort ever. Nefertiti was to bear her husband six daughters: Meritaten, Meketaten, Ankhesenpaaten, Neferneferuaten-the-Younger, Neferneferure and Setepenre. These young princesses were to play an unusually prominent role in their father's reign, while the third-born daughter, Ankhesenpaaten, was eventually to marry the pharaoh Tutankhamen. There is no record of Nefertiti ever bearing a son.

Throughout the first year of his reign Amenhotep IV was an irreproachably orthodox monarch. There was no military campaigning, but building work continued in and around the Karnak temple where the new king decorated his father's unfinished gateways. In Year 2, however, it was announced that a *sed* festival would mark the third anniversary of the king's accession. This was unusual; as we have already seen, a *heb-sed* would normally be celebrated after thirty years on the throne. Amenhotep's festival proved to be more than a simple anniversary party. Just as the celebration of his father's *sed*-festival had signalled his developing interest in the theory of divine rule, so Amenhotep IV was to use his celebrations to mark his own devotion to a new god. Now the builders set to work and Thebes—home of Amen—was soon equipped with a series of temples and cult-buildings all dedicated not to Amen but to the Aten.

The Year 3 celebrations saw Amenhotep reinterpreting the traditional rituals to exclude many of the great state gods. This was just a foretaste of

things to come. By the end of Year 5 the Aten had become Egypt's principal deity and the king had changed his name to Akhenaten, or "Living
Spirit of the Aten." As the royal offerings stopped, the traditional cults
ground to a halt and Egypt's temples closed down, their assets diverted to
the cult of the Aten. Almost two thousand years of tradition had been apparently erased in less than five years. From this point onwards history
tends to focus on the confined, claustrophobic sphere of Akhenaten's
court, and we have little idea of what went on in the "real world" away
from the centre of Aten worship.

Was this true revolution, or merely a continuance of the developing interest in solar theology and divine kingship seen towards the end of his father Amenhotep's reign? Was it a genuine religious conversion, a cynical
attempt to promote the living king's own divinity, or merely a means of
stripping Amen of his wealth and power? Was Akhenaten perhaps wor-
shipping his dead and deified father in the form of the Aten? We would certainly be naïve to simply classify this as a religious experience, and should
study Akhenaten's new faith within its political and economic context.

A new god needed a new city untainted by Amen or any other deity.
Akhenaten established his new capital, Akhetaten (today known as
Amarna or Tell el-Amarna), on a virgin site on the east bank of the Nile
in Middle Egypt, part-way between Thebes and Memphis. Here the city
was defined by a series of impressive inscriptions (boundary stelae)
carved into the limestone cliffs. By Year 9 Amarna was fully functional and
the court had retired to its permanent home. Here Akhenaten, absorbed
in his own self-created world, grew increasingly remote from the realities
of life outside Amarna.

The inscriptions on the boundary stelae make it clear that Akhenaten
intended his new city to be Egypt's permanent capital, home of the Aten
and of the state bureaucracy that until now had been centred on Memphis.
Amarna therefore included everything that a successful capital might need:
temples, palaces, offices, workshops, housing and, of course, a burial
ground including an exclusive royal section, the Royal Wadi, where the
king and his immediate family would enjoy eternal rest in the royal tomb.
The scenes carved into the rock-cut tombs of the nobles betray something
of the uncomfortable reality of Amarna life. While the royal family go

serenely about their daily affairs their people show a new obsequiousness; those who approach the king are now compelled to bend almost double. Although Akhenaten is often cited as a pacifist, these scenes suggest that he very much liked to be in control.

His isolated city had an unusually strong military presence; policemen and soldiers make regular appearances in the scenes of daily life which decorate the tomb walls while the tracks worn by the guards who patrolled the cliffs may still be seen today. We have no means of telling whether these guards were intended to protect, or to intimidate, the citizens who had been compelled to abandon their homes and family tombs to embark on Akhenaten's great adventure.

Clearly, the royal family benefitted from the change in religious practices. In material terms they were freed from the obligation to make offerings to scores of gods, and indeed they gained from the confiscation of the estates of the traditional cults. At a higher level, total control of the sole god left the king in a seemingly unassailable position. Akhenaten, perhaps learning from the precedent of the once powerful Amen priesthood, had no intention of promoting his new cult so that it was in a position to challenge or even weaken his own position. Quite the reverse: following the example set by his semi-divine father, Akhenaten consistently exploited his new god as a means of emphasizing his own, and his family's, divine role.

Now, as the tiny, faceless, disembodied sun-disc glowed in the Amarna sky, perhaps serving as a symbol for the dead Amenhotep III, the living king became the most prominent figure in any religious scene and the queen was seldom far behind. The temples to the Aten—the only places where the new god could receive offerings—allowed the high priest Akhenaten to control access to a god who, by his very nature, might otherwise have been all too easily accessible to the masses. Only the king and queen could communicate with the Aten; everyone else had to address their petitions to the king and queen.

Atenism has frequently been lauded as the world's first monotheistic religion, an intelligent, caring forerunner to Judaism, Christianity or Islam. Many of those who have read the *Great Hymn to the Aten*, a poem found inscribed in the tomb of Ay which is often assumed to have been written by the king himself, have been struck by its similarity to the biblical Psalm 104 with its references to a sole deity, the god of all life:

> Bless the Lord, O my soul.
> O Lord my God, thou art very great; thou art clothed with honour and majesty.
> Who coverest thyself with light as with a garment: who stretches out the heavens like a curtain:
> Who layeth the beams of his chambers in the waters: who maketh the clouds his chariot: who walketh upon the wings of the wind ...
>
> *Psalm 104*

> Glorious, you rise on the horizon of heaven, O living Aten, creator of life. When you have arisen on the eastern horizon you fill every land with your beauty. You are gorgeous, great and radiant, high over every land. Your rays embrace all the lands that you have made. You are Re and so you reach their boundaries, limiting them for your beloved son. Though you are far away, your rays are upon the earth. Though you are seen, your movement is not. . . .
>
> *The Great Hymn to the Aten*

However, as with all aspects of Amarna life, it is dangerous to take this one piece of evidence out of context. Many of the ideas expressed in the *Great Hymn* can be traced back to the reign of Amenhotep III, if not earlier. To class Atenism as a monotheistic religion is certainly to oversimplify matters. The Aten was never Egypt's sole god—Re, and the divine royal family, continued as objects of worship throughout Akhenaten's reign. Nor was the Aten a universal or democratic god available to all; he was determinedly exclusive and his light—made explicit by his long, thin rays— shone down for the royal family alone.

Hatchepsut had found it impossible or unwise to challenge the time-honoured image of kingship, and had felt it expedient to be depicted as a conventional male king performing traditional kingly deeds. Akhenaten had no such qualms; he was not concerned with tradition. Suddenly the once normal king is depicted in two and three dimensional relief with a curious range of physical deformities: his narrow head and stalk-like neck emphasize his almond-shaped eyes, pendulous earlobes, heavy jaw, long nose, thick lips and sharply defined cheekbones. His shoulders, chest, arms and shins are significantly underdeveloped while his jodhpur-like hips and thighs, gently rounded breasts and curved stomach give the king a classic female "pear-shape." One broken colossal statue recovered from Thebes and now housed in Cairo Museum even shows the naked king without male genitalia. These features, which in two-dimensional art make Akhenaten appear less than impressive, combine in the colossal sculptures designed to grace the temple precincts to give the king a curious, compelling quality emphasized by the sensual nature of his curved lips.

Egyptologists, art-historians and medics have been divided over the correct interpretation of these images. As archaeologist Wilfred Griggs says: "It has been thought by many people that this is the result of inbreeding and genetic mutation. Others think that this is really just a revolutionary art style. [Now, given modern scientific advances including DNA analysis,] we should be able to start attacking the issue of whether or not the Amarna Period is really the result of excessive inbreeding or genetic mutation that would have been passed on in the family."

It would certainly be wrong, given the evidence offered by Hatchepsut's statuary, to leap to the conclusion that these grotesque figures must be true to life. Egyptian art was not the equivalent of our modern photograph album; every representation was created for a specific religious purpose, and an exact likeness was far from essential. Indeed, we know that royal defects—for example the 19th Dynasty king Siptah's deformed foot and the Tuthmoside family buck teeth (defects which are known from their preserved mummies), or even Hatchepsut's femininity—were simply ignored as the artists sought to present the conventional images of regality that would reassure both mortals and gods. Here the royal sculptors were not being asked to create lifelike portraits for the guidance of future art historians, they were chiselling images to please Akhenaten and the Aten. It may be that symbolism, always latent in royal images, was now allowed to come to the fore: the king was presenting a deliberate, experimental mixture of feminine and masculine traits that would emphasize his connection with the Aten, the divine sole creator. As Egyptologist Nick Reeves has noted, there is a real danger involved in focusing on these individual pieces of art away from their original context:

> Akhenaten certainly looks strange. He is certainly not a normal-looking chap, at least in his more extreme sculptures. However, the most extreme sculptures are the colossi from Karnak which were intended to be seen from down below. Nowadays they are almost invariably photographed from the front so you have this extraordinary distortion of the chin and the face, and the lengthening. If you look at that same sculpture from below then the distortion is far less. It is still pretty weird-looking, but the impression is more one of power than of peculiarity. I think Akhenaten was making a point—the king is different.

However, if we are to take Akhenaten at face-value and seek a medical reason for his curious appearance, there are two possible causes. Several experts have suggested that Akhenaten may have suffered from Fröhlich's syndrome, a group of symptoms caused by damage to the pituitary gland. Sufferers may experience a distribution of fat over the breasts, hips and thighs and an under-development of the genitalia, and these symptoms are consistent with Akhenaten's statuary. However, men with Fröhlich's syndrome are impotent and sterile while Akhenaten, the master of a large harem, is known to have fathered many children.

An alternative diagnosis, that Akhenaten may have suffered from Marfan's syndrome, is worthy of serious consideration. Marfan's syndrome is a genetically determined abnormality caused by defective collagen formation which affects the bones and joints, leading to lengthening of the skeleton, lax joints and long fingers and toes. There may also be a high palate and eye defects but there would not necessarily be a female-type distribution of body fat. Akhenaten's face, as revealed by his statues, certainly appears to show a narrow palatal arch but, in the absence of his skeleton and skull, this cannot be proven. Perhaps the best that we can conclude, given our restricted evidence, is that Akhenaten may have allowed his artists to emphasize or exaggerate his own idiosyncratic appearance (possibly the result of illness or deformity) in order to make a theological/political point.

Several of Akhenaten's artistic "innovations" may actually be traced back to his father's reign, when Amenhotep III became the first pharaoh to be shown in all his unflattering humanity. Some of Amenhotep's later statues show the almond eyes, curved lips, sharp features and incipient breasts of the early Amarna statuary, while his final portraits show the old king as a limp and languid old man rather than an upright, perpetually young pharaoh. Does this mean that Amenhotep too may have been ill, perhaps carrying a disease that was passed on to his son? Turn-of-the-century suggestions that Amenhotep was "suffering" the effects of an unconventional, uncontrollable sexual appetite are now discredited.

Dr James Harris, geneticist and dentist, has had long experience of X-raying the skulls of the pharaohs. He has examined the head attributed to Amenhotep III, discovering that its owner must have exhibited a curious range of facial features similar to those seen in Akhenaten's statuary and portraiture, including a pointed chin and exceptionally large skull: "Amenhotep III, or the mummy identified as Amenhotep III, is extremely short, less than 5 feet [1.57 metres], yet his skull is two standard deviations too large for his body. So this was rather a bizarre-looking individual."

Unfortunately, the identification of Amenhotep's mummy is by no means certain and James Harris is careful to acknowledge this fact. Many experts now feel that the body recovered in 1898 as part of a cache stored in the tomb of Amenhotep II may have been mislabelled in antiquity. (The discovery of this mummy will be considered in more detail in Chapter 7.)

While it remains possible that Akhenaten suffered from a distorting illness, it seems highly unlikely that everyone at his court did. And yet the artistic record shows that as the king changes in appearance, so do his family and his associates. Nefertiti's face and body start to reflect those of her husband until it becomes very difficult, if not impossible, for art historians to tell the two apart unless they are wearing their distinctive crowns. This, of course, opens up the possibility that the genital-less colossal statue already discussed is, despite its royal regalia, a representation of the queen rather than of the king. It is hard to imagine that this confusion between king and queen, male and female, is anything other than deliberate. Indeed, towards the end of her life her less stylized statuary—made famous by the bust recovered from Amarna and now displayed in Berlin Museum—shows that Nefertiti was in no way deformed.

As her image evolved the queen's status, too, changed. We have already seen that Tiy, mother of Akhenaten, was allowed to play a prominent role in her husband's reign. Nefertiti was able to take things a stage further by participating in hitherto entirely male rituals. Thebes has yielded images of the queen offering as a priest to the Aten, while a block recovered from Hermopolis Magna shows her smiting the female enemies of Egypt. Nefertiti has already developed her own unique headdress, a tall, flat-topped blue crown modelled on the crown worn by Tefnut, daughter of the sun-god.

The young princesses were consistently included in family scenes where they served as a living reminder of their parents' fertility. The royal artists, struggling to convey a natural childishness never before expected of them, present the girls as miniature versions of their mother complete with good child-bearing hips and fragile limbs. As the girls wear neither wigs nor crowns, baldness emphasizes their curious elongated egg-shaped heads. Again, it is difficult to establish the "truth" behind these seemingly deformed heads. Is this evidence for a genetic problem, or proof of deliberate head-shaping during childhood? Akhenaten's own head is invariably hidden beneath an elongating crown—could he, too, have been naturally or artificially deformed? The fact that one of the girls, Ankhesenpaaten, is depicted with a normal head alongside Tutankhamen several years after her father's death suggests that, rather than attempting realism, the royal artists were making a theological point centred on the acceptance of the egg as a symbol of creation.

Akhenaten's private life was dominated by forceful women: his mother, his wife and even his daughters each had her own political and religious role to play. Now one further royal woman, Kiya, comes to prominence in the written and archaeological record at Amarna. Akhenaten is so strongly associated in the public imagination with Nefertiti that there is a tendency to forget that he also had a harem of secondary wives. Kiya's inscriptions show her to have been an important and highly favoured member of the Amarna court, but her origins remain obscure. She never claims the consort's title of "King's Wife" yet like any other high-ranking female member of the royal family she is given her own "sunshade" chapel, an honour that came with its own valuable estate. Kiya's relationship to the king is, however, obvious; we know that she bore Akhenaten at least one child as we have a relief showing the couple together with their unnamed daughter. Kiya remained in favour during the middle years of Akhenaten's reign but was absent by Year 12.

The Amarna idyll ended soon after Year 12 with the death or disappearance of many of the royal women: Kiya, dowager queen Tiy, four of the princesses and Nefertiti all vanish. From this point onwards our understanding of the 18th Dynasty royal family becomes confused as we start to suffer from a lack of written evidence. The entire pharaonic age is characterized by an absence of the intimate private records that would cast light on the personalities of the past, but at the end of the Amarna era this deficit is compounded by a shortage of official pronouncements. Akhenaten's ill-fated city was abandoned and almost entirely demolished after his death, when its stone blocks were incorporated into nearby building works. Although the ruins of Amarna have yielded some important textual information, including a fascinating collection of diplomatic correspondence that casts light on international relationships at the end of the 18th Dynasty, we have no incontrovertible evidence to help us unravel the tangled succession between the later part of Akhenaten's reign and the accession of Tutankhamen. Egyptologists, searching for clues in the royal graveyards, have yet to agree on the sequence of events leading to the end of the 18th Dynasty.

The death of Princess Meketaten is recorded on the wall of her father's partially completed tomb in the Amarna cliffs. The scene is now sadly incomplete and its accompanying inscription unreadable but, as it was copied at the turn of the century, we know that it originally referred to the "King's Daughter of his body, his beloved, Meketaten, born of the Great Royal Wife Nefertiti." The badly damaged Akhenaten and Nefertiti stand facing the bier on which rests the body of their dead daughter. Outside the chamber we see a woman nursing a child; an open fan held over the infant confirms its royal status, but this child must remain anonymous as its name has gone. The unexplained presence of a baby in such an inappropriate setting strongly suggests that we are witnessing a scene of birth and death, with Meketaten, no more than fourteen years old, dying in labour. As a teenager Meketaten would certainly not have been considered too young to marry. The question therefore needs to be asked, who was her husband? There is no obvious sign of the father of the baby at the death scene, while Akhenaten is present. This has led some observers to suggest that Meketaten may have married her father.

We have already encountered brother–sister incest in the Tuthmoside royal family, although both Amenhotep III and Akhenaten—the two pharaohs who, it has been suggested, may well have carried an inherited disease—are known to have chosen non-royal brides. Tiy's parentage, at least, is well documented, and the mummies of both her parents have been recovered from their intact tomb to provide confirmation of their daughter's non-royal lineage. The Egyptologists who first uncovered evidence for brother–sister incest in the New Kingdom royal family were shocked. Such an unnatural practice, it was reasoned, must have been forced upon the unfortunate couple. Thus the "heiress theory," the idea that the king had to wed the sister who alone could transmit the right to inherit the throne, was born. This theory, in the light of the non-incestuous marriages of Akhenaten and Amenhotep III, is now recognized as over-simplistic; marriage with a sister, assuming that there was a suitable unmarried sister available, was merely one option open to the prince consort.

Brother–sister incest was not widespread among the general population but it did offer several advantages to the royal family. First, it emphasized the fact that royalty was more closely connected with the gods, who practised incestuous marriages, than with their subjects. At a more practical level it allowed the royal family to retain its exclusivity while solving the problem of finding suitable spouses for both princesses and princes; a daughter could be raised from birth to be an effective queen just as a son could be trained to be king, and a brother–sister marriage would exclude "in-laws" who might attempt to influence or even disrupt the succession. The effect of this tradition on the royal family is difficult to assess. Inbreeding may, but does not invariably, lead to the weakening of the family line. As microbiologist Scott Woodward has summarized: "There has been a lot of speculation about the genetics of the 18th Dynasty. What was the level of inbreeding? How much brother–sister marriage did we really have, and did that cause a problem with the health of the individuals? Is that a reason why the 18th Dynasty died out? These are some questions that might be approachable using the DNA."

As we know Akhenaten's mother to have been a non-royal, we can discount the possibility that the pharaoh suffered from a disease specifically resulting from inbreeding; the introduction of Queen Tiy into the royal family would have effectively reset the genetic clock so that Akhenaten's own inbreeding coefficient would have been zero. However, there still remains the possibility that Akhenaten, like his father before him, suffered from some hereditary disease. The analysis of the royal DNA would, as Woodward suggests, help to settle this matter. Unfortunately, identifying the DNA of Akhenaten and his close relations is easier said than done.

Now it is suggested that we have evidence for father–daughter incest at Amarna, with Akhenaten accused of marrying not one but three of his daughters. As with so many aspects of Akhenaten's reign, this "new development" can be traced back to the reign of his father.

Within the late 18th Dynasty royal family the eldest princess occupied an important, if untitled, position. As the queen grew older it became perfectly acceptable for her eldest daughter to serve as consort alongside, or instead of, her mother. Thus towards the end of his reign we find Amenhotep III marrying his daughter Sitamen and elevating her to the rank of "King's Chief Wife" beside the still powerful Queen Tiy. This tradition was to continue into the 19th Dynasty, when we find Ramesses II marrying at least two of his daughters who then become queens alongside, or instead of, their mothers. In a country accustomed to the institution of the co-regency (two kings on the throne) a co-queenship made good sense. In marrying Sitamen, Amenhotep may have been emulating the solar god Re, who is known to have had a relationship with his daughter Hathor. He may also have been offering his deserving daughter the ultimate promotion from princess to queen; a promotion she would not necessarily have achieved had she been forced to marry one of her brothers and wait for her long-lived father's death.

There is no reason for us to assume that royal father–daughter marriages were not fully consummated; Ramesses II had a child by his daughter Bintanath. However, these marriages do not affect the succession; we have no recorded instance of the child of such a union inheriting the throne and cannot claim that they were undertaken as a means of conceiving an heir.

The evidence for two of Akhenaten's suggested incestuous marriages is tentative to say the least. The only evidence for his marriage to Meketaten is that found in the royal tomb: the deathbed scene with Akhenaten and Nefertiti but no husband present. Unfortunately, as we are unaware of the traditions associated with birth and death, we cannot state with any degree of certainty that we would expect to find a husband rather than a parent present at such a time. The evidence for Akhenaten's marriage to Ankhesenpaaten is even weaker. It rests almost entirely on the sudden and confusing appearance in the written record, late in the Amarna era, of two young princesses named Meritaten-the-Younger and Ankhesenpaaten-the-Younger. The parentage of these two is never explained and, although it has been occasionally assumed that they were named after their mothers and that they were therefore the product of father–daughter incest, it seems equally if not more likely that they are daughters born either to Akhenaten and Kiya or to Meritaten and Ankhesenpaaten by other husbands. The remains of these two princesses have never been recovered.

The evidence for the incestuous marriage of Meritaten is slightly stronger, although certainly not overwhelming. As Meketaten dies and Nefertiti vanishes we find Meritaten, always her father's favourite, growing in importance until she is honoured with the titles of a royal wife. The obvious implication is that, with Nefertiti dead, Meritaten has married her father and is now acting as his consort. Again, however, this sequence of events is nowhere made explicit so that the possibility always remains that Meritaten has become a royal wife by marrying someone else, a hitherto invisible co-regent of Akhenaten. We know that there was such a person around at this time; towards the end of the Amarna age Prince Smenkhkare appears as from nowhere, his parentage never explained.

Kiya, like Meketaten, may have died in childbirth. The royal tomb preserves images of a second death-bed scene paralleling that of Meketaten. In the first tableau we see Akhenaten and Nefertiti with their right arms raised in grief as they stand before something or someone now vanished, while outside the chamber a nurse is again holding a royal baby. In the next scene we see the royal couple mourning before the body of a young woman lying on a bier. Again the story seems obvious: another mother has died giving birth to a royal child. This time the dead lady is, however, unnamed. She cannot be Meketaten; her death is commemorated elsewhere. Nor can she be Meritaten or Ankhesenpaaten, as they were both to outlive their parents. The remaining sisters, if not already dead, would have been too young to themselves become mothers. It therefore seems likely, as Egyptologist Geoffrey Martin has suggested, that this is Kiya, dying as she gave birth to a royal baby. The name of the baby is not preserved.

Part-way through his reign Akhenaten took a co-regent. At approximately the same time Nefertiti, once so prominent, disappears. The obvious inference is that she too is dead; this would certainly explain Meritaten's increasing prominence within the royal family. However, we have no trace of Nefertiti's burial and no account of her funeral. To many Egyptologists this silence seems inexplicable. Surely Akhenaten would have commemorated his beloved wife's death had she predeceased him; could Nefertiti therefore have still been alive?

In the 1970s an elegant theory, developed by Egyptologist John Harris on the basis of surviving, tantalizingly incomplete inscriptions, sought to address the mystery of the vanishing queen. Harris put forward the suggestion that Nefertiti had not died, but had cast off her queenly role to become a king alongside Akhenaten, first using the regal name Ankhkheperure Neferneferuaten and then, following the death of Akhenaten, ruling alone as Ankhkheperure Smenkhkare using her eldest daughter Meritaten as queen. Finally, it was reasoned, Nefertiti, or Smenkhkare as she was now known, passed the throne to a young prince named Tutankhaten, son of Akhenaten and a secondary wife, who was by then married to her third daughter Ankhesenpaaten.

Smenkhkare's name was already known to Egyptologists but he was a disembodied being, a possible co-regent to Akhenaten and husband to Meritaten yet without proven parentage and lacking either a mummy or a tomb. Now, however, his sudden appearance at precisely the moment that Nefertiti disappeared could be explained in spectacular fashion. Nefertiti had become Smenkhkare and was now king of Egypt.

Not everyone has been convinced by King Nefertiti/Smenkhkare. The theory of her co-regency very much hinges upon the question of whether or not Smenkhkare was a real person. So far, the evidence that we have considered can be read either way. There need be nothing sinister in Smenkhkare's lack of background. This is precisely what we would expect from a New Kingdom prince and, indeed, it is exactly what we have already seen happening when the hitherto invisible Akhenaten ascended to the throne. If Smenkhkare was not a child of Akhenaten and Nefertiti, but a child born to a lady of the harem, we would not expect him to play any prominent role in the royal family until his destiny was assured.

The evidence suggested by the royal names is by no means conclusive, the order of use not necessarily fixed. Given the propensity of the Amarna royal family to change their names to fit with their current religious beliefs, it does not seem unreasonable to suggest that Smenkhkare, Ankhkheperure Smenkhkare and Ankhkheperure Neferneferuaten may be one and the same, male, person. However, it is equally reasonable to trace the evolution of Nefertiti via her more lengthy name Neferneferuaten-Nefertiti into Ankhkheperure Neferneferuaten and finally Ankhkheperure Smenkhkare.

Nor is precedent any help in determining the chain of events. As we have seen, the women who had previously ruled Egypt were almost invariably the mothers of pharaohs too young to take their throne. Just twice, during the Middle Kingdom reign of Sobeknofru and the New Kingdom reign of Hatchepsut, had a woman managed to rule alone; in both these cases, the female kings were members of the royal family by birth. Never had there been an instance of a queen being promoted to rule alongside a king. The closest parallel to Nefertiti is probably that offered by Queen Tiy, a lady who, although she showed unprecedented influence throughout her husband's reign, never actually became co-regent.

Of course, lack of precedent does not necessarily disprove the Nefertiti-as-Smenkhkare theory; there was much about the Amarna Period that did not follow precedent. However, human remains recovered from a small rock-cut tomb in the Valley of the Kings pose a more serious objection by furnishing the hitherto ephemeral Smenkhkare with a possible body. The mummy from Tomb KV 55, and its relationship to Tutankhamen, will be discussed further in Chapters 7 and 8.

Towards the end of his reign, perhaps incensed by the deaths of his nearest and dearest, Akhenaten intensified his campaign against the old priesthoods. He died of unknown causes after seventeen years on the throne, leaving Egypt demoralized and significantly weakened, her empire all but gone. His religious revolution had been a failure. Within five years the old gods would be restored, the Aten retreated into obscurity, and Amarna abandoned as Tutankhaten, once a very peripheral figure, ruled Egypt from Thebes and Memphis as the pharaoh Tutankhamen.

CHAPTER SEVEN

Who?
The Lost
Pharaohs

> Excitement had gripped us hitherto, and given us no pause for
> thought, but now for the first time we began to realize what a
> prodigious task we had in front of us, and what a responsibil-
> ity it entailed. This was no ordinary find, to be disposed of in
> a normal season's work; nor was there any precedent to show
> us how to handle it.
>
> Howard Carter

CAIRO MUSEUM IS NOW HOME TO OVER THIRTY MEMBERS OF THE EGYPTIAN
royal family, including many of the 18th Dynasty kings and their consorts.
Today visitors to Cairo may gaze upon the faces of some of the world's
most famous rulers, still recognizably human after almost three and a half
thousand years. Meanwhile, secure within his outer coffin and sarcophagus, in his tomb in the Valley of the Kings, lies the body of Tutankhamen,
now the most famous of all the pharaohs.

The unique collection of ancient human tissue housed in Cairo Museum allows Egyptologists and scientists the opportunity to confirm and even expand the New Kingdom dynastic history, discussed in Chapter 6, which has been derived from more traditional archaeological and textual sources. It may even help to untangle some of the complexities that mar our understanding of the end of the 18th Dynasty. For example, DNA analysis may be able to prove or disprove the popular theory that the royal family suffered from a hereditary disease that eventually brought about their demise.

But how have so many royal mummies escaped the attentions of the tomb robbers? The answer lies in the Valley of the Kings.

Eighteenth Dynasty Thebes was a city of two contrasting halves. The east bank was the land of the living: here could be found the mud-brick palaces, offices, workshops, warehouses, houses, slums and even the "Great Prison" which once signalled a thriving community but which are today lost beneath the ground water. Here, too, on higher ground and built in stone, were the imposing temple complexes of Karnak and Luxor where Amen, "The Hidden One," and his divine family dwelt alone in the splendid darkness of their sanctuaries.

Across the river lay the land of the dead: the Redland housing the well-guarded, rock-cut tombs of the pharaohs and their courtiers plus the more humble cemeteries of the wider population. Standing at the interface of life and death, on the very edge of the desert, were the west bank mortuary temples, the cult centres built by each living king to function as a temple of Amen during his lifetime and a temple to the deceased merged with Amen after death. The west bank, although effectively an extensive necropolis, was not necessarily a hushed or a morbid place. Indeed, the constant building projects, the communities of workmen, the daily funerals and the divine and commercial traffic to and from the mortuary temples, ensured that the floodplain shared some of the hustle and bustle of the eastern city. To escape from humanity it was necessary to climb to the remote, forbidden Valleys of the Kings and Queens.

The Old Kingdom Egyptians, destined to spend eternity within the tomb, had packed their graves with the goods that they felt they would need after death. These ranged from the essential (food, wine and clothing) through the sentimental (heirlooms, favourite tools and pots) to the amusing (cosmetics, perfumes, jewellery and games). Only the poorest members of society went to the grave empty-handed. Even pharaoh, the one Egyptian who confidently expected to leave his pyramid to dwell for ever with Re, was buried with a vast array of precious items. Not surprisingly, thieves were attracted to Egypt's graveyards like flies to a corpse. By the 18th Dynasty the pyramids were open and empty, the royal mummies almost entirely vanished.

New Kingdom theology was more democratic; a reflection of a society that now included a substantial, economically significant middle class. Now everyone was allowed to leave the tomb and, as the soul would no longer be trapped on earth, the only grave goods necessary were protective amulets and the papyrus scrolls that acted as the official guidebook to the Afterlife. However, old funerary traditions die hard. We know from the virtually intact burial of Tutankhamen that the corridors and chambers of the rock-cut tombs were still stuffed with precious objects: a combination of ritual goods—items such as shabtis, or model servants—and consumer items that the spirit might use within the tomb. The New Kingdom monarchs knew that their burials—or rather the precious items within their tombs—would attract thieves, but they were not prepared to abandon their grave goods and golden coffins. Even Akhenaten, who as a follower of the Aten should have shunned the old Osiris-based funerary rituals, allowed his undertakers to provide mummification, coffins, shabti figures, magical bricks and grave goods for the Amarna dead. Needless to say, Egypt's tomb robbers continued to prosper.

Naturally, the pharaohs sought to protect their graves against the thieves who threatened their chance of eternal life. It was well known that those caught robbing the tombs could expect little mercy. Stealing from the dead, and casually destroying mummified bodies, was a heinous offence striking at the very survival of the soul of the deceased. The courts were empowered to award the harshest of punishments: the guilty might be impaled on a stake, mutilated, or sent off to serve a life sentence in one of pharaoh's work gangs.

Prevention was, however, better than cure. Secrecy was obviously the best line of defence, but it was recognized that total secrecy was impossible. No one could hope to build a rock-cut tomb in secret, and so secrecy had to be combined with a policy of strict necropolis security. The Valley of the Kings, a suitably remote site, was guarded at all times. The small, dedicated workforce who built the royal tombs were well paid and well respected. They lived together, apart from the rest of the Theban population, in the walled west bank village of Deir el-Medina. Here the one gateway to the village allowed government officials to search those entering and leaving the complex. While the state bureaucracy flourished, this system worked well and the royal tombs were protected for hundreds of years. However, towards the end of the 20th Dynasty, the unified Egypt started slowly to disintegrate. Economic instability, high inflation and official corruption caused delays in the issuing of rations, leading to a series of strikes on the west bank. The Deir el-Medina workers, unpaid and dissatisfied, started to make use of their secret knowledge, targeting the nearby temples and tombs.

By the end of the New Kingdom the royal necropolis had become so insecure that Ramesses XI, the last king of the New Kingdom, abandoned his Theban tomb and returned to Memphis. Now, as Deir el-Medina too was abandoned, its once valued workmen stripped of their status, the royal tombs were left vulnerable and exposed.

The Third Intermediate Period saw a strife-torn southern Egypt ruled by the high priests of Amen based at Thebes. By now most of the royal tombs had been entered and robbed many times, but there were still pickings enough to attract undesirable looters to the west bank. The priests therefore decided to take pre-emptive action and to seize any remaining valuables for themselves. The royal tombs were officially opened and their contents removed to a series of temporary workshops established in the mortuary temples and empty tombs. Here the loot was sorted. All valuable items were confiscated for recycling; they would make a much needed contribution to state coffers depleted by years of fighting. The royal mummies, efficiently stripped of all remaining amulets and jewels by the priests, were rebandaged as necessary, housed in plain wooden coffins and then stored in empty tombs. From time to time, perhaps because they continued to attract thieves, the mummies were inspected, restored and moved. Eventually the necropolis held two major royal collections: one stored in the Pinodjem family vault at Deir el-Bahari and one in the tomb of Amen-hotep II in the Valley of the Kings. As thirty centuries flowed by, the royal mummies were forgotten.

The first westerners to explore the Valley of the Kings searched in vain for an intact royal burial. They found plenty of regal tombs, but all were disappointingly empty with only their elaborately decorated walls and empty sarcophagi to hint at the splendours they once may have held. Then in 1871 Ahmed Abd er-Rassul, a member of a family of notorious tomb robbers living in the west bank village of Gurna, discovered the concealed entrance to the Deir el-Bahari cache. Legend has it that Ahmed stumbled across the shaft while hunting for a lost goat—although given his family business, it seems equally likely that he was actually searching for tombs to rob. Selling antiquities was, of course, illegal then as it is now, but the tourists who flocked to Luxor (modern Thebes), and the unscrupulous dealers who had extensive contacts with western museums and collectors, regarded this as little more than a legal technicality.

Ahmed and his brothers Hussein and Mohammed exploited their amaz-ing discovery, targeting not the denuded New Kingdom pharaohs but the intact burials of the Pinodjem family. For ten years they were able to live off the contents of the tomb. However, as the antiquities market became flooded with exquisite Third Intermediate Period funerary papyri, the au-thorities grew increasingly suspicious. It was obvious that a new tomb had been discovered, and imperative that they too locate the tomb before it was completely emptied.

Suspicion was bound to fall on the Abd er-Rassul family; rumours of their spectacular good fortune were already circulating and everyone in Luxor knew where to go to buy a really good papyrus. Eventually Mo-hammed was forced to reveal the whereabouts of his treasure trove, and an incredulous Emile Brugsch, the representative of the Egyptian Antiqui-ties Service, became the first Egyptologist to be lowered down the wide shaft, squeeze through the doorway and creep along the low, right-angled corridor, easing past the coffins that threatened to block his way. At the end of the corridor a brief flight of steps led downwards into a storeroom. Here, by the light of his candle, Brugsch came face to face with Egypt's missing kings.

His words were quoted by E. Wilson writing in *The Century Magazine* in 1887: "Their gold covering and their polished surfaces reflected my own excited visage so that it seemed as though I was looking into the faces of my own ancestors. The gilt face on the coffin of Queen Nefertari seemed to smile upon me like an old acquaintance. I took in the situation quickly, with a gasp, and hurried to the open air . . ."

Expecting to find a Third Intermediate Period tomb, Brugsch had in fact discovered a New Kingdom cache. Here, among kings from the 17th to the 20th Dynasty, lay the 17th Dynasty Sekenenre Tao II, the 18th Dynasty Ahmose, Queen Ahmose-Nefertari, Amenhotep I and Tuthmosis I–III and the 19th Dynasty Ramesses I, Seti I and Ramesses II. Beyond this store-room a second, higher corridor led to a chamber holding the substantially intact Pinodjem family burials. Brugsch had the tomb cleared immediately, without pausing to photograph or plan the chamber, and within two days the first of the mummies were sailing northwards to Cairo Museum. Here the more important of the kings were put on display, while the remainder went into store.

Although the Deir el-Bahari cache had gone a long way towards repopulating the empty tombs of the Valley of the Kings, it was obvious that many well-known pharaohs were still lost, presumably stored in a different cache or caches. The archaeologists now knew what they were looking for. In February 1898 a team led by Victor Loret discovered the robbed tomb of Tuthmosis III in the Valley of the Kings. A month later, while his workmen were still busy clearing Tuthmosis' tomb, Loret uncovered another hidden doorway. Among the broken and discarded grave goods surrounding the tomb entrance was a shabti figure bearing the name of Amenhotep II.

Loret and his foremen clambered into the tomb and half slid, half crawled downwards into the darkness. With the aid of a ladder they crossed the well that threatened to bar their way, and found themselves in a pillared hall. Here, in Loret's own words, the flickering light revealed a horrible sight. Amid the debris of a thoroughly looted tomb, on a broken wooden boat: "A body lay there upon the boat, all black and hideous, its grinning face turning towards me and looking at me, its long brown hair in sparse bunches around its head. I did not dream for an instant that this was just an unwrapped mummy. The legs and arms seemed to be bound. A hole exposed the sternum, there was an opening in the skull . . . ." (*Les Tombeaux de Thoutmes III et d'Amenophis II*, Cairo, 1899).

This was indeed an unwrapped mummy which, robbed and stripped of its bandages while still tacky with embalming unguents, had been flung by robbers into the funerary boat where it had stuck for thousands of years.

The passageway continued downwards leading through two further chambers to an impressive columned hall. Here in a wooden coffin within an open sarcophagus lay Amenhotep II himself, his funerary wreath still in place. His was not, however, an original burial. Amenhotep had been restored during the Third Intermediate Period when other mummies had been stored in his tomb. Now a side chamber yielded three mummies lying side by side, while a large sealed side room held nine further royal mummies in wooden coffins including the 18th Dynasty Tuthmosis IV and Amenhotep III.

The three mummies recovered from the side chamber have been the subject of intense Egyptological debate. Although they were initially classified by Loret as a man, a long-haired woman and a laughing boy, the "man" was nothing of the kind. The anatomist Grafton Elliot Smith in *The Royal Mummies* (1912) rather witheringly corrects this case of mistaken identity: "The examination of this mummy yielded the most surprising results because M. Loret had described it as a man's body, whereas it required no great knowledge of anatomy to decide that the excellently preserved naked body is a young woman's. . . . The only reason I can assign for such a curious and obvious mistake is the absence of hair on the head. All the hair had been clipped very short or shaved."

The "man" was re-named the "Younger Lady" to distinguish her from her burial-mate. The "Elder Lady," although unlabelled, is now thought by many to be Queen Tiy. This body, complete with long, flowing hair, had been bandaged in a quasi-regal pose with her left arm bent in front of her chest. A strand of the mummy's hair has been matched to a lock of hair labelled with Tiy's name and included among Tutankhamen's grave goods. While this once seemed to offer conclusive proof that the mummy was indeed Tiy, the accuracy of the analytical technique has recently been queried and the identity of the mummy is once again open to question.

Tiy is not, of course the only missing 18th Dynasty queen; Nefertiti, Meritaten and Ankhesenamen all remain to be discovered, while there are some who would identify the "Elder Lady" as Hatchepsut. However, the Deir el-Bahri cache, which included an anonymous New Kingdom female body, has also yielded a decorated wooden box bearing Hatchepsut's name and titles and housing a preserved liver or spleen, which suggests that the female pharaoh may not have been sent to the Amenhotep II cache.

With Loret's discovery, the sequence of 18th Dynasty monarchs was almost complete. Initially, all the mummies were left in the tomb. Next Amenhotep, the body in the boat and the three stripped mummies in the side chamber were put on display in the tomb (the body in the boat suitably protected with chicken wire), while the remaining mummies were sent to join the collection in Cairo Museum. However, after a disastrous robbery which led to the disappearance of the boat plus its body and the stripping of the mummy of Amenhotep II, the decision was take to transfer the whole collection to Cairo. Back in Thebes Howard Carter, then Inspector General of the Monuments of Upper Egypt, was able to trace the footprints of the robbers to the house of Mohammed Abd er-Rassul. The brothers stood trial for tomb robbery, but were acquitted.

The bandages and coffins of the mummies had been labelled in hieratic script by the Third Intermediate Period priests who supervised their restoration. It is solely on the basis of this labelling that we are able to put names to the otherwise anonymous kings and queens recovered from the Theban caches. Of all the royal mummies it is only Tutankhamen, recovered from his own intact burial, who can be unequivocally identified as himself. Of course, Egyptologists cannot be blind to the danger that the priests may have confused their royal charges. While some of the kings appear exactly as we might have expected (the mummy identified as the nonagenarian Ramesses II, for example, is obviously the mummy of a very old man), others are less convincing. In particular, the badly damaged mummy attributed to Amenhotep III, father of Akhenaten, is thought by some to have been misidentified. The mummy attributed to Tuthmosis I, although exhibiting a family likeness to the other Tuthmoside kings, is likely, on the basis of the positioning of the arms which are shielding his genitals rather than crossed on his chest, to be the remains of his non-royal father, Ahmose

Sipairi. Unfortunately this well-wrapped mummy with no areas of exposed and damaged skin is not currently available for the DNA testing which might have provided additional clues to its identity.

In contrast, the mummy of the 17th Dynasty Sekenenre Tao II, the father of Ahmose, believed to have died fighting the Hyksos, offers definite confirmation of this king's last moments. First unwrapped by Egyptologist Gaston Maspero in 1886, and then re-examined by Grafton Elliot Smith in 1906, the body showed horrific wounds and evidence of hasty mummification, perhaps on the field of battle. Smith described it in *The Royal Mummies*: "No attempt was made to put the body into the customary mummy-position; the head had not been straightened on the trunk, the legs were not fully extended, and the arms and hands were left in the agonizing attitude into which they had been thrown in the death spasm following the murderous attack, the evidence of which is so clearly impressed on the battered face and skull."

Sekenenre Tao had been killed by a blow to the skull from a Hyksos battleaxe.

While we have no proof that the priests ever mixed up their mummies, we can certainly prove that they confused their coffins. Close inspection of the Deir el-Bahari cache revealed several surprises: the coffin of the 18th Dynasty Queen Ahmose-Nefertari, for example, also held the 20th Dynasty Ramesses III, while Ramesses II was in a coffin originally designed for his grandfather, Ramesses I. The 18th Dynasty Queen Ahmose-Inhapy lay in the coffin the 18th Dynasty royal nurse Rai while Rai's own body was retrieved from the coffin of the 21st Dynasty Paheripedjet. Most confusing of all was the case of Tuthmosis I, discovered lying in a nest of two coffins, one belonging to Pinodjem I and one of his own which had been adapted for use by Pinodjem and then rejected. Pinodjem himself was found in a second Tuthmoside coffin.

Today, unwrapping mummies is seen as a destructive process to be performed only on bodies threatened by decomposition or fungal infection. It is an exact, time-consuming science performed by multi-disciplinary teams, and a full unwrapping may take weeks or even months to complete. In the late nineteenth century, however, things were very different. Mummies were unwrapped very much as a matter of course—there was little consideration given to the right of the deceased to remain bandaged. While the public unrollings that had so entertained Belzoni's audiences were largely a thing of the past, the unwrapping was still performed with a certain degree of showmanship, albeit showmanship disguised as science. In Cairo Museum Tuthmosis III became the first of the Deir el-Bahari kings to be subjected to this indignity.

The king's shroud and bandages had already been attacked by the Abd er-Rassul brothers, who had burrowed through his chest in a search for the valuable heart scarab which would have been placed within the mummy wrappings by the ancient undertakers to act as a magical substitute heart. Then Emile Brugsch had unwrapped and rewrapped the king in 1881, discovering the four wooden paddles that the Third Intermediate Period restorers had incorporated in the wrappings as stiffening. Now, in 1886, it was the turn of Gaston Maspero, Director of the Egyptian Antiquities Service, to slice through the bandages and re-expose the badly damaged pharaoh.

Tuthmosis, once Egypt's greatest general, was in pieces. His hands were still folded across his chest but all four limbs and his head had been detached in antiquity. When reassembled, the king was found to have stood some 1.615 metres (about 5 feet 3 inches) tall, with a large head, buck teeth and a narrow, high-bridged nose. He appeared to have died in his late fifties; an age entirely consistent with his fifty-four-year reign. While the remains of the original 18th Dynasty bandages were still stuck to the king's skin, his body was now covered with what Maspero identified as an unpleasant "layer of whitish natron charged with human fat, foetid and strongly caustic."

Twenty years later Grafton Elliot Smith also gained access to Tuthmosis III. He found that the king's face, protected by a covering of ancient resin, was well enough preserved to attempt to reconstruct the appearance of the "Egyptian Napoleon." Smith, in his excellent *Royal Mummies*, compared the mummy to images of Tuthmosis preserved at Hatchepsut's Deir el-Bahari mortuary temple:

> The mouth is slightly opened and the lower lip is drawn outwards. The forehead is very low. The small gracefully moulded ears have preserved their form. It is not possible to say for cer-

tain whether the lobule is pierced.... No trace of hair or beard can be found anywhere on the head, excepting the eyebrows and a very few short white hairs just behind the left ear. Thoutmosis [Tuthmosis] III was almost completely bald.

From 1968 onwards the royal mummies housed in Cairo Museum were examined by a team from the University of Michigan School of Dentistry, working in conjunction with the University of Alexandria under the guidance of James Harris. The team used a combination of conventional X-rays and cephalometrics—radiographs which, taken with a precise orientation, facilitate the taking of measurements and the comparison of one mummy to another, thereby allowing the identification of family groups. This work broadly confirmed Smith's earlier observations; the investigators were able to identify a family resemblance between Tuthmosis, his father Tuthmosis II, grandfather Tuthmosis I (or great-grandfather Ahmose-Sipairi) and son Amenhotep II. Tuthmosis III had been a short man of medium build whose well-spaced teeth showed some wear but no decay. This dental pattern is typical of ancient Egypt, where there was little sugar to cause caries, but where wind-borne sand made its way into food causing intense abrasion leading, in the most severe cases, to abscesses.

However, the suggested X-ray age at death of thirty-five to forty years for Tuthmosis III is obviously incompatible with both the historical records, which allow the king a reign of at least fifty years, and the findings of other investigators using more traditional anatomical studies.

This is not the only instance where X-ray analysis has suggested an unacceptably early age for a mummy. The "Elder Lady" recovered from the tomb of Amenhotep II, generally accepted by anatomists as being in her mid-forties, is accorded an X-ray age of twenty-five to thirty years. If correct—and many would consider this to be a big if—this age would make her too young to be either Tiy (known as queen for at least thirty-eight years) or Hatchepsut (reigned twenty-two years; queen for at least three years and probably longer before her accession)—although not too young to be Nefertiti. Most puzzling of all is the calculated X-ray age of the 19th Dynasty Ramesses II, who has a well-documented reign of sixty-six years and yet who apparently died aged fifty to fifty-five! Clearly, and assuming that the bodies have been correctly identified, there is something seriously wrong with this method of dating ancient bones.

The most recent investigation into the mummy of Tuthmosis III has been conducted by a team from Brigham Young University, Utah, working with Nasry Iskander, official in charge of the Cairo Museum mummies. For a few years Dr Iskander has been overseeing the restoration and transfer of twenty-seven of the fragile royal bodies from their old, inadequate wooden boxes to new display units designed to imitate the preserving conditions of their tombs. The new cases will protect the mummies against fluctuations in temperature, humidity, oxygen level, pressure, vibrations, bacterial action and the harmful rays of the sun. Once safely sealed in their environmentally controlled, nitrogen-rich, airtight cases the royal mummies will not be disturbed again for many years. The move therefore offers an excellent, and perhaps the last, opportunity to collect tissue samples for scientific analysis from the royal mummies.

Microbiologist Scott Woodward and Wilfred Griggs, archaeologist and Coptic expert, have developed an expertise in the extraction of ancient DNA by working in the extensive post-dynastic desert cemetery of the Egyptian Faiyum where, for at least a thousand years (approximately 500 BCE to CE 500), local families buried their dead. This cemetery, currently under excavation, is estimated by Griggs to hold between half a million and a million bodies. Here Woodward and Griggs have been able to identify family groups on the basis of the genetic information contained within their bones. This most intimate data, combined with the archaeological evidence, has allowed the excavators to address otherwise insoluble questions posed by the cemetery: are the clusters of burials family units? Is there any evidence for incestuous marriages within the community? Any evidence of changing population? Was the population threatened by hereditary disease?

Now, Dr Iskander hoped that Griggs and Woodward could use their DNA expertise to investigate the genetic history of the 18th Dynasty. As Scott Woodward recalls:

> We actually started genetic analysis with the cemetery population to see whether or not it was in fact possible to recover an-

cient DNA from individuals that lived two and three thousand years ago, and also whether or not it was possible to understand population genetics; whether or not we could reconstruct genealogies. There were things that we were able to demonstrate in the cemetery which we can now transfer directly to the work that we are doing with the royal mummies.

The team, being careful not to damage the mummies, have been able to extract small tissue samples from within the body cavities which, it is hoped, have not been in contact with more modern human DNA. This work is still in progress and is as yet unpublished, but already it has proved possible to confirm some of the long-known documented facts about the 18th Dynasty. The DNA profile makes the dynastic break between Amenhotep I and Tuthmosis I obvious, while the continuation of the royal line from Sekenenre Tao to Ahmose, across the artificial 17th–18th Dynasty divide, is also very clear. The evidence for inbreeding, brother–sister incestuous marriages, is strong at the beginning of the dynasty but is not apparent at its end; it seems that whatever brought about the end of the 18th Dynasty, it was not excessive inbreeding.

Eight years after Loret's discovery of the Amenhotep II cache, a 1906–7 expedition led by the British Egyptologist Edward Ayrton and financed by the American lawyer and keen amateur archaeologist Theodore M. Davis stumbled across the modest entrance to the tomb now known as KV 55. In plan, KV 55 was simple: a single burial chamber reached via a sloping corridor. The contents of the tomb were, however, far from simple; they baffled their discoverers in 1906 and continue to baffle today's Egyptologists who are somewhat frustrated in their attempts to understand the archaeology of the tomb by the shortage of proper plans and a detailed publication.

The newly discovered burial chamber was a chaotic mess, with wooden boxes, mud bricks, stone chips and the tools of the ancient workmen strewn all over the floor. The whole collection was dusted with a glittering flaking of gold leaf that had floated from the decaying remains of a gilded shrine propped against the walls. Amid the jumble was a golden inlaid coffin which, in the absence of a stone sarcophagus, had originally rested on a wooden bier that had long since collapsed on to the floor. Beneath the dislodged coffin lid the archaeologists could see a mummy and, in a recess in the right-hand wall, they saw four human-headed canopic jars.

The disorder in the burial chamber and the curious nature of the grave goods and workmen's debris suggested that the sealed tomb had been breached, investigated and possibly robbed by the workmen excavating the overlying tomb of Ramesses IX. However, the mummy, usually the first target of thieves searching for valuable amulets and jewels, still lay intact in its coffin. The contents of the tomb, variously bearing the names of Amenhotep II, Amenhotep III, Tiy, Akhenaten and Tutankhamen, dated it to the later 18th Dynasty. The tomb could not have been closed before Tutankhamen's accession and, as his was the last name associated with the tomb, it appeared likely that it had been finally closed during his reign. There was, of course, always the possibility that this was the reburial of someone who had died elsewhere in an earlier reign.

Included within the tomb were a set of magical funerary bricks bearing the name of Akhenaten; these would normally be included among the king's own burial equipment where, placed at the four corners of the burial chamber, they would have offered protection to the deceased. Also present was the dismantled golden shrine, part of the burial equipment of Queen Tiy provided by her son; "The King of Upper and Lower Egypt, living on truth [Akhenaten], that he made for the king's mother, the Great King's Wife Tiy." Akhenaten's image had been erased from the shrine but Tiy remained beneath the Aten's rays. The shrine had been designed to be erected around the sarcophagus of the dead queen. Unfortunately, when discovered it was in a very fragile condition, and it fragmented before it could be properly recorded.

The four canopic jars bore ill-fitting, and therefore possibly not original, stoppers carved with delicate female heads wearing the Nubian-style bobbed wigs favoured by many of the higher-ranking women at the Amarna court. Again, the name of the original owner had been erased, but it seems, on stylistic grounds, that the stoppers at least must have belonged to Akhenaten's favourite, Kiya.

The bare walls of the tomb offered no clue as to either its intended or its actual occupant. The anthropoid (human-shaped) coffin, which under normal circumstances might have furnished the name of the owner, was a mass of conflicting clues. The measurements and design of the coffin indicated that it had been built for a woman and, as its head had been designed to wear a wig rather than a crown, it seems safe to assume that this was a non-royal woman. However, at a later stage the coffin had been fitted with a beard and uraeus (the symbolic cobra on a monarch's headdress), making it suitable for the burial of a royal male. The uraeus and the gold mask that covered the face had then been torn off in antiquity, leaving the underlying wood exposed. It seems that the coffin, originally built for a non-royal lady, was later adapted for use by a royal male whose name, but not necessarily whose mummy, was defaced in antiquity.

This reading of the coffin is confirmed by the text on the foot-end and the bands of hieroglyphic decoration. These were originally written as words to be spoken by a woman, someone who could describe herself as the beloved of Waenre (Akhenaten) and as the "perfect little one of the living disc." However, these inscriptions had been altered from feminine to masculine, while the name of the original owner had been replaced by a name in a cartouche, which was itself later erased. It is reported that the inscribed golden bands recovered within the mummy wrappings bore the name of Akhenaten, but these were unfortunately stolen before they could be properly recorded.

On the basis of this evidence, it seems reasonably safe to conclude that the coffin and the canopic jar stoppers, if not the jars themselves, had originally been intended as part of the burial equipment provided for an important Amarna Period lady: Kiya is the obvious choice. However, there is no evidence that they were ever used as such. Some time later, before the end of Tutankhamen's reign, they were adopted for use by an unidentified royal male—presumably the body in the coffin.

At first sight the mummy seemed well preserved. Theodore Davis watched as it was unceremoniously stripped:

> Presently, we cleared the mummy from the coffin, and found
> that it was a smallish person, with a delicate head and hands.
> The mouth was partly open, showing a perfect set of upper
> and lower teeth. . . . Rather suspecting injury from the evident

dampness, I gently touched one of the front teeth (three thousand years old) and alas! it fell into dust, thereby showing that the mummy could not be preserved. We then cleared the entire mummy . . . .

The Tomb of Queen Tiyi (London, 1910)

Unfortunately, water dripping from a crack in the ceiling had fallen directly into the open coffin, rotting both mummy and coffin, while the skull had been further damaged by a fall of rocks. The coffin could be restored, but the mummy was beyond repair. The hasty unwrapping was never properly recorded and the mummy, now reduced to a skeleton, was eventually sent to Cairo Museum where it remains today. We will return to this mummy in Chapter 8.

By the time that Howard Carter started his work in the Valley of the Kings in 1917, most of the New Kingdom pharaohs had been recovered and the general consensus was that the Valley had little more to offer. One king, however, was still missing. The young pharaoh Tutankhamen had never been found, although his embalming cache—the discarded refuse of the royal undertakers—had been discovered in the valley in 1907 by a team of archaeologists funded by Theodore Davis. Tutankhamen was a short-lived, somewhat insignificant figure and, Carter reasoned, his burial may have been overlooked by both robbers and restorers. Sponsored by Lord Carnarvon, he started a systematic survey of the Valley of the Kings in a painstaking, and highly extensive, search for the missing pharaoh. By 1921, however, Carnarvon was losing faith in the project. The partners agreed that the 1922–23 season was to be their last.

The story of the momentous discovery of Tutankhamen's tomb (KV 62) has been told and retold so many times that it is familiar even to those with no interest in ancient Egypt. Howard Carter was of course proved right. Tutankhamen's tomb had been preserved by accident: hidden underneath tons of rubbish dumped during the 20th Dynasty excavation of the slightly higher tomb of Ramesses VI. Theodore Davis had, in fact, come very close to discovering the lost tomb; in 1914, on one of his many missions to the valley, he had stopped digging a mere couple of metres (about six feet) from the hidden entrance.

On November 4, 1922, Carter's workmen uncovered the first of sixteen steep stone steps leading downwards to a sealed doorway. Excitedly, Carter stopped work and telegraphed to England: "At last have made a wonderful discovery in Valley; a magnificent tomb with seals intact; re-covered same for your arrival; congratulations."

Lord Carnarvon arrived in the Valley of the Kings on November 23. Now, as the clearing of the stairwell resumed, the name of the tomb owner was at last confirmed by the sealings on the door. The tomb was unquestionably that of the lost pharaoh Tutankhamen and, although there were the unmistakable traces of re-sealing indicating that the tomb had been breached in antiquity, Carter remained optimistic that the tomb was substantially intact. Once again his optimism was to prove well founded. The thieves, although they had stolen maybe a sixth of the king's jewellery, had not managed to penetrate to the burial chamber. And necropolis officials, alerted to the break-ins, had been able to restore and re-seal the tomb before it suffered too much damage.

The corridor beyond the outer door was blocked with limestone chips, through which the ancient thieves had burrowed. The chips had to be removed and sifted for archaeological clues, so that it was not until November 26 that the team reached a second sealed door. Here Carter made a small hole and, holding a candle before him, put his head in—and saw those "wonderful things."

The archaeologists clambered through the door and marvelled at what they saw. The next day electric lights were installed, the plan of the tomb was determined, and clearance work started in the antechamber.

KV 62, like KV 55, was a simple tomb; not the elaborate burial place of a long-lived king but a private tomb adapted for a pharaoh whose own tomb was perhaps unfinished at his death. The west wall of the antechamber included the sealed entrance to the annexe, another storage area, while the north wall led via a sealed doorway to the plastered and painted burial chamber and a fourth room, the treasury, beyond.

Unlike the impetuous Davis, Carter was a patient man well-trained in the new science of excavation. Aware that he was dealing with a unique discovery, he intended to do the job properly no matter how long it took. The antechamber, a jumbled warehouse of grave goods that had been disturbed by thieves and tidied by necropolis officials, had to be cleared of its treasures before Carter could proceed to the burial chamber. Here in precarious heaps were stacked animal-headed beds, chariot parts, stools, boxes, baskets and much, much more. Here too, against the north wall, stood two life-sized guardian statues protecting the sealed doorway to the burial chamber. After seven weeks of hard work, of planning, recording, photographing, removing and conserving, the antechamber was clear and the official opening of the burial chamber could take place (with the Queen of the Belgians invited to watch as guest of honour).

Within his burial chamber the dead king lay at the heart of a concentric puzzle of coffins, sarcophagus and shrines. The outermost shrine, an ornate gilded wooden structure inlaid with brilliant blue faience, almost completely filled the chamber. Unbolting its folding doors, Carter discovered a gilded wooden frame holding a fragile linen pall spangled with golden daisies. The shrine beyond this still bore the seal of the dead king: proof that the ancient thieves had not managed to penetrate this far. As Howard Carter was later to recall: "Henceforth, we knew that, within the shrine, we should be dealing with material untouched and unharmed since the boy king was laid to rest nearly three thousand years ago."

Two further shrines were to be unbolted before the enormous yellow quartzite sarcophagus, carved from a single block of stone, was revealed. Here was the king, protected by the goddesses Isis, Nephthys, Selket and Neith, who stood with outstretched winged arms to guard the four corners of his sarcophagus. Then all progress stopped. It was necessary to dismantle and remove the shrines before the broken sarcophagus lid—of red granite painted yellow to match the base—could be lifted.

Tutankhamen was discovered lying within a nest of three anthropoid coffins resting on a bier. The outermost coffin was of cypress wood modelled with a thin layer of plaster and covered with gold foil. The middle coffin was of an unidentified wood covered in gold and inlaid with glass and precious stones. Finally, the innermost coffin was of solid gold, its beauty somewhat marred by a "thick black pitch-like layer of resin"—the remains of the anointing liquid poured over the coffin during the funeral and now effectively gluing the innermost coffin into the base of the middle coffin. As Carter recalled, "This pitch-like material hardened by age had to be removed by means of hammering, solvents and heat, while the shells of the coffins were loosened from one another and extricated by means of great heat, the interior being temporarily protected during the process by zinc plates, the temperature being employed though necessarily below the melting point of zinc was several hundred degrees Fahrenheit."

Within the coffin the mummy, too, had been anointed, although the beautiful gold mask that covered the face had been deliberately avoided so that it still glowed with its ancient polish.

CHAPTER EIGHT

How?
The
Evidence
of the Bones

The youthful Pharaoh was before us at last: an obscure and ephemeral ruler, ceasing to be the mere shadow of a name, had re-entered, after more than three thousand years, the world of reality and history. Here was the climax of our long researches! The tomb had yielded its secret; the message of the past had reached the present in spite of the weight of time, and the erosion of so many years.

Howard Carter

TUTANKHAMEN'S WAS NOT THE ONLY BODY TO BE RECOVERED FROM TOMB KV 62. In the chamber known as the treasury, Carter discovered an undistinguished wooden chest (box 317) housing two small black and gold anthropoid coffins, the lids of which had been tied in place with linen strips and sealed. When opened, each coffin yielded a golden inner coffin holding the perfectly mummified body of a premature baby. While the smaller mummy wore a gilded cartonnage (a *papier maché* mix of plaster and papyrus or old linen bandages) face mask, the mask provided for the slightly larger mummy had evidently proved too small to fit over the bandaged head; rejected by the undertakers, it had been buried with the king's embalming material. Here Davis had found it in 1907.

Carter himself removed the bandages of the smaller mummy before, in 1932, inviting Douglas Derry, Professor of Anatomy at Cairo University, to conduct an autopsy on the tiny body. Derry found the body to be that of a premature girl, of maybe five months' gestation, some 25.75 centimetres (10 inches) long, with part of the umbilical cord still in place. The body had been dried with natron, but there was no sign of the embalming cut that would show it had been eviscerated first.

The larger mummy was also female, this time a baby of approximately seven months' gestation, some 36.1 centimetres (14 inches) long. The umbilical cord had been cut but the stump had not had time to shrivel away, suggesting that the baby may have died at, or soon after, birth. This baby had been eviscerated through a cut on the left side, and the skull had been filled with natron-impregnated linen.

Nowhere are we told the identities of these two little girls. The gilded inscriptions on their outer coffins simply refer to them as "the Osiris," a conventional way of referring to the Egyptian dead. However, it is clear that these were children of some importance. The undertakers had gone to a great deal of trouble, and expense, to preserve the tiny bodies. While this does not rule out their inclusion in the tomb for unknown, ritual purposes, the obvious conclusion is that they are the short-lived children of Tutankhamen and his wife Ankhesenpaaten, the third daughter of Akhenaten and Nefertiti who was now known as Ankhesenamen. We know that 18th Dynasty children were occasionally included in their parent's tomb, and we have already seen Meketaten being buried in her father's tomb at Amarna. If these are two premature sister-princesses, they are our last known link with the family of Tutankhamen and Akhenaten. As it is now official policy not to disturb Tutankhamen in his tomb, they offer our only chance of obtaining tissue samples from this branch of the family.

Both foetuses are today stored in the Department of Anatomy, University of Cairo, where they rest in the boxes and cotton wadding provided by Howard Carter; they remain in excellent condition under the care of Dr Fawsi Gaballa, Professor of Anatomy. Meanwhile their coffins are now part of the collection in Cairo Museum.

X-ray examination of the two foetuses led Professor Robert Harrison of Liverpool University to suggest that the larger of the two babies may have suffered from Sprengel's deformity, with spina bifida and scoliosis or curvature of the spine. He also felt that this child might have been born at full term. More recently the Utah team have been able to extract minute tissue samples from both bodies for DNA analysis. While it has not been possible to extract a genetic profile for the smaller foetus, the larger baby has yielded a mitrochondrial DNA sequence through which the scientists may be able to trace the maternal DNA of Ankhesenamen and her mother, Nefertiti. Work on this material is still in progress, but so far it has yielded no sign of any genetic disease or congenital deformity that might have caused the end of the Tuthmoside royal line.

Three years after the discovery of the body of Tutankhamen, the autopsy was performed in the tomb of Seti II in the Valley of the Kings, with the king still resolutely stuck in the base of his innermost coffin. It had been intended that the king would be X-rayed before the unwrapping, but the radiographer had unfortunately died on his way to the tomb and the project was to be postponed for forty years. Now Professor Derry was entrusted with the delicate task of unwrapping Tutankhamen and detaching him from his casket. Derry made his first cut on November 11, 1925, working before an invited audience of Egyptologists and officials.

Beneath the resin-coated shroud the king's bandages had been almost completely carbonized, making it impossible to determine the precise order of wrapping. It was clear, though, that the fingers, toes and limbs had been individually wrapped while the penis had been bound in an erect position. The arms had been bent at the elbow to cross the chest, with the left arm lying on top of the right. The chemist Alfred Lucas, present at the unwrapping, believed that this carbonization was due to a natural spontaneous combustion perhaps exacerbated by the presence of fungus. However, Howard Carter's notorious use of intense heat to separate the nest of coffins may well have contributed to this disaster.

Derry removed the decayed bandages from the feet upwards until the entire torso was exposed; the king was then dismembered to allow his removal from the coffin. Finally the golden mummy mask was removed with the use of hot knives, and the king's face was revealed for the first time in over three thousand years. Tutankhamen appeared as a young man, clean shaven, his nose flattened during mummification, and with pierced ears.

Derry was able to confirm that Tutankhamen had died a young man of slight build, standing some 1.63 metres (5 feet 4 inches) tall. Tutankhamen's unfused long bones indicated that he had been approximately eighteen years old at death. The evidence of the long bones is always important in the ageing of a skeleton. Initially, in childhood, the ends of the long bones are separate from the main shaft of the bone and are linked by cartilage. As the individual grows the long bones grow too, until eventually the end of the bone fuses as adult stature is reached. Gradually, then, the lines of fusion fade away. Derry was unable to suggest a cause of death, but he did note that Tutankhamen's slightly elongated skull was very similar in shape to the anonymous skull found in Tomb 55.

In 1968 Robert Harrison, working in conjunction with dental expert F. Filce Leek, was allowed to X-ray Tutankhamen's skull and body within his tomb. The results of this analysis confirmed Derry's observations regarding the king's youth—indeed, Leek believed that Tutankhamen may have been as young as sixteen when he died—and skull shape, and were able to disprove the old theory that Tutankhamen might have died of tuberculosis. Ten years later James Harris was able to obtain cephalometric X-rays of the king; again Harris agreed with the diagnosis of Derry and Harrison. Thus, in a rare case of experts and historical evidence (Tutankhamen having a recorded reign-length of less than ten years) all in agreement, we can conclude first that Tutankhamen died after a brief reign in his late teens of no immediately obvious cause, and secondly that he had a head very similar in appearance to the KV 55 skull.

The X-rays made it clear that part of the king's ribcage was missing, presumably lost in the embalming house. It was also possible to observe a detached piece of bone, loosened during the embalming process, lodged in the skull cavity. With no obvious cause of death, and no sign of any inherited genetic disorder, it seems reasonable to suppose that Tutankhamen may have died in an accident which caused damage to his chest; even today, accidents are a prime cause of death among young men. Alternatively, the suggestion has been put forward by Tutankhamen expert Bob Brier that the young king may have died following a deliberate blow to the back of the head. Examination of Harrison's skull X-ray, at the point where the head meets the neck, shows a misted area of thickening which, although considered by Professor Harrison to be well within the normal range, may indicate an old wound. Assuming that this is indeed evidence of a fatal blow, and assuming again that this blow was deliberate rather than accidental, it has been suggested that Tutankhamen may have been assassinated, either by the followers of the courtier Ay, or the followers of the general Horemheb; both were subsequently to rule Egypt as pharaoh.

The body, by now a skeleton, recovered from Tomb 55 has since its 1907 discovery been at the centre of an intense archaeological and anatomical debate. Although there was nothing about the mummy itself to confirm that it was a member of the royal family, its burial in the Valley of the Kings, and the archaeological evidence within the tomb, strongly suggested that this was a late 18th Dynasty body in some way connected with the Amarna court. The published reports of the stripping of the mummy are both brief and uninformative, and as the operation was conducted without the benefit of photographs we can make little comment on the bandaging of the body. Nevertheless, from the account left by Edward Ayrton we can compile the image of a small person, wrapped with the left arm bent with the hand on the breast and the right arm straight with the hand on the thigh; this, half-way between the crossed arms of the pharaoh and the straight arms of the commoner, is a standard royal female pose seen in statuary, and has already been found in the "Elder Woman" recovered from the Amenhotep II cache.

Theodore Davis, aware of the inscriptions on the golden shrine recovered from the same tomb and perhaps influenced by the positioning of the mummy's arms, was convinced to his dying day that he had discovered the body of Queen Tiy. The two "experts" whom he summoned to confirm his theory, a local doctor and an American obstetrician holidaying in Luxor, left him in no doubt that the body was female, and it was as the *Tomb of Queen Tiyi* that he published a record of his work.

However, Grafton Elliot Smith, far more experienced in the study of ancient bones, disagreed and indeed no one has since classed the bones as female. To Smith, the first anatomist to examine the bones, the body was clearly male, the remains of a young man of about twenty-five years of age. Akhenaten was known to have reigned for seventeen years, and to have fathered children during the first years of his reign. This suggests that he must have been at least thirty years old, and probably at least five years older, when he died; he would therefore have died too old to be the KV 55 mummy. Nevertheless, many read Smith's diagnosis as confirmation that the mummy was indeed that of Akhenaten himself. Smith, obligingly extending his age-limit upwards, wholeheartedly agreed, writing in 1912 in *The Royal Mummies*:

> From the circumstances under which the coffin and human remains were found, in association with many inscribed objects bearing the name of Khouniatonou [Akhenaten], which also appeared not only on the coffin itself but also on the gold bands encircling the mummy, there can no longer be any doubt that the body found in this tomb was either that of the heretic king, or was believed to be his corpse by the embalmers. . . . I do not suppose that any unprejudiced scholar who studies the archaeological evidence alone would harbour any doubt of the identity of this mummy, if it were not for the fact that it is difficult from the anatomical evidence to assign an age to this skeleton sufficiently great to satisfy the demands of most historians, who want at least thirty years into which to crowd the events of Khouniatonou's eventful reign. . . . If we accept the generally admitted criteria, this skeleton is that of a man about twenty-five or twenty-six years of age . . . if, with such clear archaeological evidence to indicate that these are the remains of Khouniatonou, the historian can produce irrefutable facts showing that the heretic king must have been twenty-seven, or even thirty,

years of age, I would be prepared to admit that the weight of
the anatomical evidence in opposition to the admission of that
fact is too slight to be considered absolutely prohibitive.

The archaeological evidence—the royal coffin with its defaced names
and Akhenaten's magical bricks—was certainly not inconsistent with this
interpretation of the body. Akhenaten, it was speculated, had died and
been buried at Amarna. During the reign of Tutankhamen, either at the
time when Amarna was abandoned or following a foiled robbery, he had
been transferred to the Valley of the Kings where he could be properly
guarded. At some point his coffin, but not his mummy, had been attacked
to remove all trace of the now hated Atenism. However, this interpretation
of events did raise certain questions—were we to assume, for example,
that Akhenaten had, at the end of a lengthy reign which would have allowed him ample opportunity to prepare for death, originally been buried
in Kiya's second-hand coffin? And why was Tiy's shrine included in the
tomb—had she too been buried here, before being transferred to a different resting place and perhaps ending up in one of the royal caches?

It seems obvious that KV 55 did not represent a primary, undisturbed
burial even before it was defaced in antiquity. The condition, type and
arrangement of the artefacts within the tomb make this clear. The tomb
therefore represents the reburial of funerary artefacts retrieved from
Amarna some time before the end of Tutankhamen's reign. This transfer
and re-burial of royal mummies, although a curious custom to modern
eyes, is well documented during the 18th Dynasty. Perhaps the most extreme known example is that of the unfortunate Tuthmosis I, who was
moved and re-moved throughout the reigns of Hatchepsut and Tuthmosis III. Unfortunately, it is not safe to assume that the contents of KV 55
represent the remains of a single burial; it seems equally, if not more, valid
to regard them—including the mummy and its coffin—as a collection
gathered from several Amarna burials and re-interred in one tomb. It is
therefore dangerous to rely on the presence of either the magical bricks or
the coffin when attempting to put a name to the mummy.

By no means everyone was convinced that the mummy was an older
man. When, in the 1920s, Douglas Derry examined and restored the re-

mains he was very doubtful that this could be Akhenaten. To him the un-fused long bones and evidence from the teeth (an unerupted right upper third molar) showed that their owner could have been no more than twenty-five years old at death. Professor Harrison, re-examining the bones in 1963, came to the same conclusion. The remains were those of a male less than twenty-five years old who had shared the same blood group (A2 and MN) as the well-provenanced Tutankhamen and Thuyu, mother of Queen Tiy, and who had exhibited the same slightly elongated head-shape as Tutankhamen.

Derry had already highlighted the similarity between the Tutankhamen and KV 55 heads. More recently James Harris has also, using computer-ized tracings, been able to show that the two heads are very close in shape with their similar jaws and cranial bases making them the closest match of all the measured 18th Dynasty royal skulls: "My conclusion is that they are first degree relatives, therefore they would be possibly a father or a son or a brother. We have no reason to believe historically that Tutankhamen had a son, so the assumption must be then a father or a brother."

Harris concluded that the bones were those of a man aged between thirty and thirty-five years, older than the age suggested by Smith, Derry and Harrison.

No one—archaeologist or anatomist—disputes that the body is that of a close relative of Tutankhamen. Much, then, depends upon the age at death of the KV 55 mummy. If the bones are those of a young man, he is likely to have been Tutankhamen's brother. The most obvious candidate for this role is the ephemeral Smenkhkare, the prince who makes a fleet-ing appearance to rule alongside Akhenaten at the end of the Amarna age and who disappears as Tutankhamen comes to the throne. To prove that the bones are those of a young man would necessarily disprove the Ne-fertiti as regent theory; we can only accept Nefertiti as Smenkhkare while Smenkhkare himself is absent.

If, however, the bones are those of an older man, a man of thirty or more, he is most likely to have been Tutankhamen's father. Tutankhamen nowhere makes his parentage known but it seems safe to assume that he was of royal blood. Without the authority of birth, it would have been vir-tually impossible for him to become a child pharaoh; Tuthmosis I and

Ramesses were both adopted as heir apparent to the Egyptian throne, but only after long, successful military careers. While there are several possible candidates for the role of royal parents (Tiy and Amenhotep III, Sitamen and Amenhotep III, Akhenaten and Nefertiti, Akhenaten and Kiya) the most obvious father, the one most consistent with the dating evidence, is Akhenaten himself. Akhenaten is known to have reigned for seventeen years, Tutankhamen for maybe nine before dying in his late teens. Tutankhamen was therefore born during Akhenaten's reign, and the only way that we could allow Amenhotep III to be his father is if we envisage a very long Amenhotep–Akhenaten co-regency. So far, there is no historical evidence to justify this assumption.

If Tutankhamen had been born at Amarna, the son of Akhenaten, he could easily have been eight or nine years old at his father's death. As Nefertiti appears not to have produced a son, the most obvious mother would then be Kiya, Akhenaten's favourite throughout the Amarna period. If this reconstruction is correct, the poignant death scene already considered in the Amarna royal tomb may well have recorded Kiya dying as she gave birth to Akhenaten's son, Tutankhamen.

The most recent analysis on the KV 55 bones has been conducted by leading British physical anthropologist Joyce Filer. She too has confirmed that the skeleton is that of a male and, having examined both bones and teeth and studied X-rays, has concluded from the state of fusion of the bones and the recently erupted back teeth that the remains are those of a younger man: "It [the skeletal evidence] points to somebody perhaps no more than mid-twenties; certainly, by the teeth I would even go younger than that." Furthermore, she has concluded that the body shows no sign of any inherited genetic disorder, although there is always the possibility that there is a recessive genetic metabolic disorder, invisible to the naked eye.

The consensus of expert opinion is therefore clear. The bones are those of a young man, almost certainly those of the lost elder brother of Tutankhamen, Smenkhkare. By making this identification we have dismissed the old theory that Nefertiti ruled Egypt alongside her husband as the pharaoh Smenkhkare and, while this does not automatically exclude Nefertiti from ruling with Akhenaten under a different name, the lack of supportive evidence makes it more reasonable to assume that Nefertiti predeceased her husband at Amarna. Both Tutankhamen and his brother appear entirely normal, with no sign of any inherited disease that might have hastened the end of the Tuthmoside line.

ABOVE: Golden mask from Tutankhamen's coffin. (*Richard Reisz*)

BELOW: The young king Tutankhamen depicted on his throne under the solar disk of the Aten with his queen, his half-sister Ankhesenamen. (*Richard Reisz*)

ABOVE: The coffins of the foetuses found in Tutankhamen's tomb by Howard Carter, as originally photographed. (*The Griffith Institute, Ashmolean Museum, Oxford*)

RIGHT: The two female foetuses – the last of the 18th Dynasty royal line? (*The Griffith Institute, Ashmolean Museum, Oxford*)

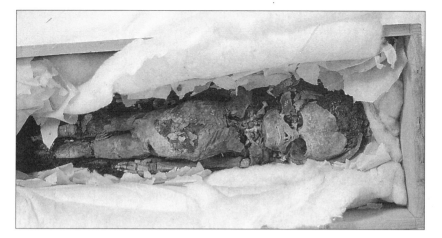

ABOVE: Nearly eighty years after the newly discovered foetuses were encased in cotton wrapping by Howard Carter, they were subjected to DNA analysis. *(Richard Reisz)*

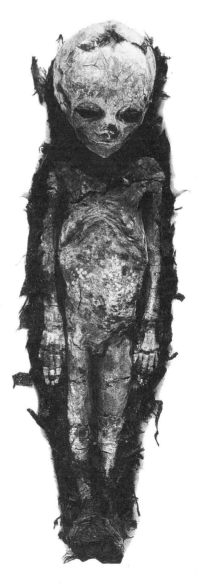

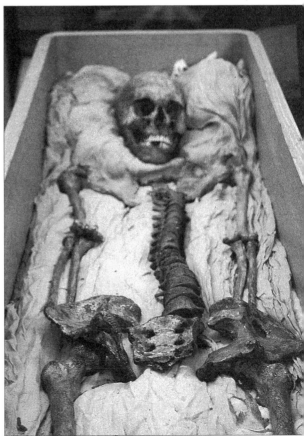

ABOVE: Within tomb KV 62, Howard Carter cleans the golden coffin of Tutankhamen. (*The Griffith Institute, Ashmolean Museum, Oxford*)

RIGHT: The skeleton from KV 55 is examined, along with other 18th Dynasty royal mummies, at Cairo Museum. (*Richard Reisz*)

ABOVE: Theban tomb painting depicting a chantress of Amen shaking a sistrum. Asru may have played a similar instrument as part of her temple duties. The blue lotus flower can be seen at the bottom left of the picture. (Richard Reisz)

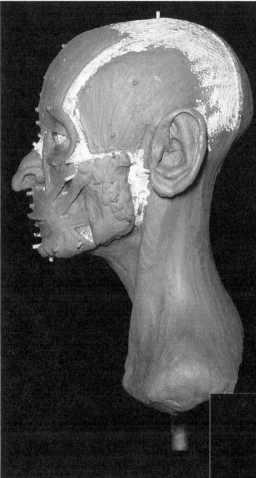

ABOVE, RIGHT AND FAR RIGHT: Once a cast of Asru's skull had been taken, experts at Manchester University were able to carry out a reconstruction of how she looked at the time of her death. (*Caroline Wilkinson, University of Manchester*)

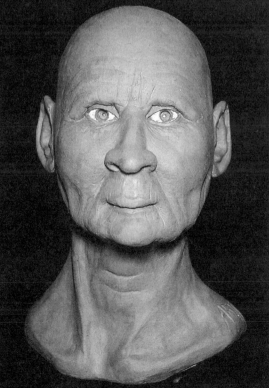

ABOVE: Tomb depictions of the blue lotus frequently show ancient Egyptians enjoying its potency, but was it as a narcotic or merely for its scent that they valued this mysterious flower? *(Richard Reisz)*

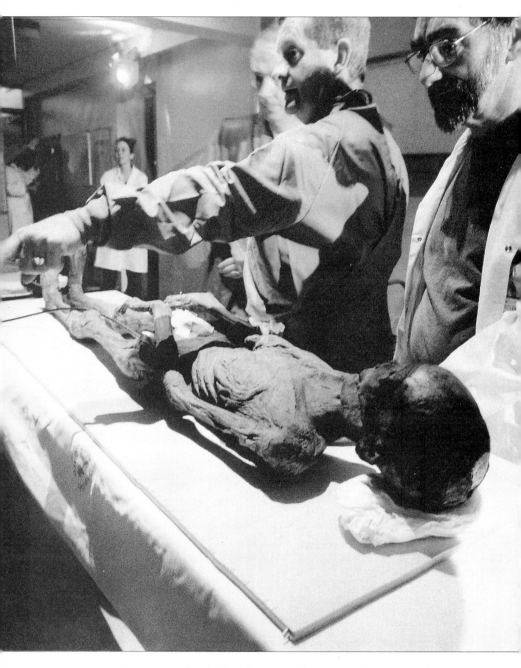

ABOVE: The mummified body of Asru undergoing endoscopy and X-ray analysis at Manchester University. (*Nigel Hillier*)

CHAPTER NINE

Why?
The
Ending
of an Era

When his majesty arose as king the temples of the gods and
goddesses, beginning from Elephantine down to the marshes of
the Delta, had fallen into decay, their shrines had fallen into des-
olation and become ruins overgrown with weeds...the gods
had turned their back on the land.

> Extract from the restoration stela of Tutankhamen,
> translation after Sir Alan Gardiner

THE EVIDENCE OBTAINED FROM THE BONES IN KV 55, COMBINED WITH THE
archaeological data already extracted from this tomb, allows the Egyptologist to turn detective and attempt a speculative reconstruction of the last
days of the Amarna court. Only further discoveries will confirm or deny
the accuracy of this reconstruction.

By Year 12 Kiya, favourite of Akhenaten and mother of the heir presumptive Smenkhkare, his younger brother Tutankhamen and at least one daughter if not two (Meritaten-the-Younger and Ankhesenpaaten-the-Younger), had died in childbirth at Amarna. Now, as the masons set to work, chiselling Kiya's name off her monuments and substituting the name and titles of Meritaten, the tombs in the Royal Wadi, although unfinished and undecorated, were pressed into use as a wave of unexpected deaths devastated the royal family. The undertakers worked overtime as Meketaten, Neferneferuaten, Neferneferure, Setepenre, Tiy and Nefertiti died and were prepared for eternal life. Although these burials have left little trace in the archaeological record, we may assume that Nefertiti and Tiy at least would have been buried in gold coffins complete with all the paraphernalia suited to the interment of an influential and long-lived queen.

Meritaten, the most prominent female figure at the Amarna court, was by now married to her half-brother Smenkhkare. He in turn had assumed the role of co-regent with Akhenaten, his marriage and co-regency being political moves designed to make obvious Smenkhkare's right to inherit the throne even though he was an heir born not to the queen but to a lady of the harem. The co-regency lasted for several years before Akhenaten died and was buried with all due ceremony, as he had always intended, in the royal tomb at Amarna.

The Amarna tomb of the official Meryre II shows us the royal family during this transitional phase. Here, on the south wall of the main chamber, is an early scene showing the old royal family: Akhenaten, Nefertiti and five of the six princesses. On the later-dating, unfinished and damaged north wall we see the new royal family. A king and queen stand without children beneath the rays of the Aten. The cartouches that identify this royal couple are now vanished, hacked out of the wall by thieves, but as they had already been recorded during the 19th century we can state with confidence that they read "King of Upper and Lower Egypt, Ankhkheperure son of Re, Smenkhkare" and "King's Great Wife Meritaten."

Smenkhkare continued to rule from Amarna, but his was to be a short and undistinguished rule. Brief though his reign had been, preparations for his funeral were already well in hand. We know that the royal workshops had, as a minimum, prepared four golden canopic coffins for

Smenkhkare because these were later to appear in the burial of Tutankh-
hamen with the name of their original owner, "Ankhkheprure," partially
erased. It has also been suggested on stylistic grounds that Tutankhamen's middle coffin, which does not resemble his other two in facial features, may well have come from the assemblage prepared for his brother.
Smenkhkare died, apparently of natural causes and, as the king and
queen had no living heir, it was Smenkhkare's young brother, Tutankhaten, who buried the king in the Royal Wadi and so assumed the crown
of Egypt.

Tutankhaten was just nine or ten years old at his accession, and already
married to his half-sister Ankhesenpaaten in a mirroring of the political
Smenkhkare–Meritaten marriage. The young king must have had guidance in the earlier part of his rule. Had he had a living royal mother, her
regency would have been automatic. Instead, Tutankhaten was supported
in his rule by courtiers inherited from his father's reign, the most prominent of whom was his step-grandfather (and grandfather-in-law) Ay. For
three or four years, possibly for the time that Tutankhamen was considered a minor, the new king ruled from Amarna following very much in
Akhenaten's footsteps, although with a gradual dilution of his father's
more extreme views. Then, with no reason given, the court suddenly
moved. From now on, for the remainder of the dynasty, Egypt would be
ruled as she always had been, from Thebes and Memphis. It was now that
the king and queen abandoned their given names to remove the reference
to the Aten, becoming Tutankhamen, "Living Image of Amen," and
Ankhesenamen. The rejection of the Aten, and reconciliation with Amen,
had begun.

As the Aten was demoted to its original, relatively minor role in the state
pantheon, the old cult temples were officially reopened and Egypt was
once again a polytheistic nation. Tutankhamen immediately developed a
politically astute allegiance to Amen. At Karnak he erected a large text,
known today as the "restoration stela," which proclaimed his devotion to
the traditional deities. Here he stressed his intention to restore *maat*
throughout the land. Tutankhamen was set to become a traditional New
Kingdom pharaoh in the time-honoured mould: a brave warrior, an efficient administrator and a diligent priest. In death he was to be buried in

the Theban necropolis alongside his respected ancestors. The contrast between his reign and the reign of his father was to be obvious to all.

At the start of Tutankhamen's rule Amarna had been home to a sizeable population of Egypt's élite but, as it became clear that the court would not be returning, numbers dwindled until the city was deserted. The nearby workmen's village, home to those who toiled in the necropolis, lasted for slightly longer. Temporarily abandoned as the court required its masons to work in the Valley of the Kings, the village was to be reoccupied and even expanded before finally closing during Horemheb's reign.

The move away from Amarna meant that the cemeteries, including the rock-cut tombs of the nobles and the tombs in the Royal Wadi, would have to be abandoned. As everyone knew that these graves were stuffed with valuables, the necropolis officials could not simply walk away. If the royal burials were to be saved from the thieves who would surely strike, there were two choices: either the cemetery could be guarded, day and night, or the tombs could be emptied and their contents moved to the relative security of the Valley of the Kings. For a while the first option was adopted, but this was both costly and, in the end, fruitless. Away from public scrutiny, the burials were easy targets. Tutankhamen, who had already turned his back on the Amarna experiment, decided to open and empty the royal tombs that meant little to him. Setting a precedent that was to be followed later by the Third Intermediate High Priests of Amen, the state coffers—or rather the king himself—were to benefit from the operation to empty the necropolis.

By now, most of the royal burials had been looted and the mummies stored in the royal tomb were possibly damaged beyond redemption. These were now abandoned to their fate as the royal workmen set to work gathering up the remains of the burial equipment and transferring it to the royal workshop at Thebes. Tutankhamen was concerned over the fate of just one body, that of his brother who, as a pharaoh, would have been accorded the dignity of his own tomb.

Smenkhkare was retrieved, rewrapped if necessary, and then moved to Thebes where he was buried together with an ill-assorted funerary assemblage made up of the less valuable items recovered from the royal tombs. His own gold coffin and gold canopic coffins were, along with anything else of value, confiscated; Smenkhkare was now to be buried in an elaborate but relatively cheap non-royal coffin used first by Kiya and then adapted for the king himself. The royal workmen inserted Smenkhkare's names into the cartouches that now adorned Kiya's coffin but, some time before the tomb was lost from view, this evidence of complicity in the Amarna regime was torn away. Smenkhkare was to be allowed to rest as the brother of Tutankhamen, but he was not to be identified with his heretic father. During the 20th Dynasty Smenkhkare's burial was to be further disturbed, and plundered, by the workmen engaged in the building of the overlying tomb of Ramesses IX.

It may be that Tutankhamen was concerned over the fate of another Amarna body. The inclusion of a lock of Tiy's hair in his own funerary assemblage, and the rescuing of her gilded shrine, suggests that he may have been willing to preserve the memory of the grandmother who connected him with the court of the glorious, and highly respectable, Amenhotep III. The fate of Tiy's body is as yet unclear. Was it already badly damaged, or was it brought to Thebes to be re-interred alongside either Smenkhkare (and subsequently moved) or Amenhotep III, or even in its own, separate, tomb? As yet the identification of Tiy with the anonymous female mummies recovered from the royal caches remains problematic. It is to be hoped that one day scientific analysis will allow us to establish a genetic link between one of these mummies and Tutankhamen himself.

Ankhesenamen gave birth to at least two still-born female children but no living son. Then, unexpectedly, Tutankhamen died after a mere nine years on the throne. His death was not the result of an inherited disease caused by generations of inbreeding, but may well have been the result of an accident. Tutankhamen's regal tomb was not yet ready, and so the young king was buried in a private tomb, possibly the tomb that Ay was preparing for himself. Ay, having presided over Tutankhamen's funeral, then became king of Egypt. The Tuthmoside line had ended.

Ay was an elderly man at his accession, and he had reigned for a mere four years before General Horemheb took the throne. King Horemheb, an astute and experienced politician, benefited from a long reign that allowed him to do much to correct the royal neglect of the Amarna Period. Horemheb's final gift to Egypt was to appoint Ramesses I, the first king of the 19th Dynasty, as his successor. Horemheb and his successors were not prepared to tolerate the memory of the Amarna age. In a persecution that continued into the reign of Ramesses II, a determined effort was made to erase all signs of Akhenaten's unconventional rule. This denial of the past was a device that would allow pharaoh to rewrite history so that the Amarna period had never existed. Alongside Akhenaten, Smenkhkare, Tutankhamen and Ay, too, were to be deleted from Egypt's history so that the official line of kings recorded in her temples now jumped from Amenhotep III to Horemheb.

Part Four

▲ ▲ ▲ ▲ ▲ ▲

The Chantress and the Lotus

The
Chantress
and the Lotus

They are not just dry, dusty bodies to us; they are full of
potential.

> Dr Rosalie David, Curator of Egyptology, Manchester
> Museum, and leader of the Manchester Museum project

THE CARVED AND PAINTED TOMBS OF THE DYNASTIC AGE ALLOW MODERN OB-
servers to catch a glimpse of a vanished world. Here we see Egypt's upper
classes as they go about their daily business. The élite are invariably healthy,
carefree and relaxed; the men tanned from their work outside the home,
the women pale, interesting and sheltered from the sun. Dressed in their
finest white garments, sparkling with jewels and cosmetics, they appear im-
pervious to the ailments and disappointments that plague more humble be-
ings. Only in the more minor figures who occasionally intrude on these
scenes do we meet the sick and the disabled, the ugly and the old.

Of course, we cannot take these vibrant images at face value. The tomb walls must be read as multi-layered messages whose meaning, upon close inspection, becomes increasingly obscure. At their most obvious level the scenes preserve the image, not of the living Egypt, but of the Afterlife anticipated beyond death. They therefore represent the hopes and ambitions of the tomb owners who long to dwell for ever in the parallel Egypt ruled by the god of the dead. In the kingdom of Osiris everything is perfect, including the body and mind of the deceased. Beyond this level Egyptologists have been able to identify recurring symbolic themes, most if not all of which seem to be connected with sexuality and the need for regeneration beyond death. Many questions, however, remain to be answered. Why are the élite invariably depicted as young and fertile? Why do they drink copiously yet seldom eat? And what is the significance of the beautiful blue lotus flower that graces so many tomb scenes?

If we are to learn about the health of the ancient Egyptians it is obvious that we need to ignore their art and turn instead to their mummified remains. The Egyptians believed that it was necessary to preserve the corpse for all eternity. This unique theology led directly to the development of artificial mummification, a practice initially reserved for the wealthiest members of the community, but which grew increasingly widespread as the dynastic age progressed. By the end of the New Kingdom the middle and upper classes routinely mummified their dead, and it was only the poorer and more rural members of society who went to their grave unbandaged. As a result, thousands upon thousands of mummies were stored in Egypt's tombs. Although many of these mummies have been destroyed, enough have survived to present a unique human tissue data-bank providing information both about the individual and the health of his or her society.

In October 1999 a multi-disciplinary project was established under the leadership of Dr Rosalie David, Curator of Egyptology at Manchester Museum, to study the mummified remains of a chantress named Asru (collection number 1777). Asru had been a wealthy citizen of Thebes living during the Third Intermediate Period. Her precise dates are uncertain, although it has been suggested that she was born some time between 700 BCE and 900 BCE. Like many women of her class, Asru worked as a chantress or singer in the Karnak temple of Amen. Dying an elderly lady, she had most probably been buried in the west bank Theban necropolis. In 1825 Asru became the first mummy in Manchester Museum when she and her two anthropoid coffins were donated to the museum by the private collectors E. and W. Garratt.

Asru makes an ideal candidate for scientific investigation. Dying at a time when the embalmer's art had reached its peak, she has been exceptionally well preserved and still has remarkably good skin for someone almost 3000 years old. Having already been unwrapped by her nineteenth-century owners, her lack of bandages makes her fully accessible; there is no need for the investigating team to cause further damage as they go about their work. As her entrails were preserved in a bundle stored between her legs, Asru's internal organs are available for examination. Finally, her painted and inscribed coffins provide us with the background details which (assuming that they do indeed belong to Asru) allow us to reconstruct her life with a fair degree of accuracy.

Over the past twenty-five years Asru had been the subject of a series of scientific investigations, but there were still questions regarding her health and her use of drugs that remained to be answered. Now she was to be re-examined in Manchester Royal Infirmary using the most modern medical techniques including X-ray analysis, CAT-scans, endoscopy and facial reconstruction. The bio-medical examination of Asru's body, and the identification of her previously unsuspected ailments and parasitic infestations, adds a whole new dimension to our understanding of ancient Egyptian society. This understanding may, in turn, prove helpful to the scientists and medics who continue to do battle against water-borne parasitic infestation in modern Egypt. As for Asru herself, the recognition of the diseases that blighted her later years helps us to gain a more rounded understanding of the realities of daily life as a pampered Egyptian lady.

As Rosalie David mused at the beginning of the project: "We know quite a lot about Asru because we have the inscriptions on the coffin, so that we can actually see her as an individual. . . . Unfortunately, there is also a great deal that we don't know about the mummy, so we are hoping that the tests that we are going to do will fill in some of these gaps."

CHAPTER TEN

When?
A Brief
History of
Mummification

There are men in Egypt who practise the art of embalming and
make it their business.

Herodotus, *Histories*, Book 2: 86

WE DO NOT KNOW WHAT PROMPTED THE EGYPTIANS TO DARE TO THINK THAT
they could ward off the natural forces of decay and decomposition and
preserve their corpses for eternity. However, we may guess that the idea of
artificial mummification was developed in the prehistoric desert cemeteries. Here, perhaps when a new pit grave was being dug, a long-dead body
would occasionally be uncovered. Lying on their sides, curled as if sleep-
ing, these coffinless corpses had their skin, hair and even fingernails intact. They had been saved by natural desiccation: the immediate contact

between the body and the hot, sterile sand inhibited putrefaction by providing an anaerobic environment that would wick fluids away from the corpse. This drying left the ancient dead darker in colour and much lighter in weight, but still recognizably human.

For as long as the Egyptians continued to bury their dead in simple desert graves, mummification remained an entirely natural process. However, as society grew increasingly materialistic, as wooden coffins, stone sarcophagi and lined burial chambers were introduced into the graves of the wealthy, the corpses became separated from the sand and, now surrounded by air, Egypt's élite started to decompose.

This was unfortunate. Already, the idea that the dead body must be preserved as an earthly home for the soul had become a basic tenet of funerary theology. While many aspects of religious belief underwent subtle changes as the dynasties progressed, this fundamental principle was to persist until the arrival of Christianity began to displace the old religious beliefs in the third century CE. The inevitable decay of the bodies was therefore recognized as a disaster that would, if uncorrected, prevent the deceased from achieving eternal life. It would, of course, have been possible to preserve the bodies by abandoning the new tomb furniture and returning to the simple, sandy pit grave, but the élite were reluctant to spend eternity trapped in a sand-filled hole. Instead, centuries of experimentation started as the undertakers sought to replicate artificially the natural desiccation that they knew could be achieved in the desert sands.

The earliest attempts at artificial mummification were entirely cosmetic. The undertakers were able to preserve the shape of the body by binding it with layers of tight, resin-coated linen bandages, using padding to give the limbs a natural, rounded appearance and plaster to mould the features of the face. However, there was no removal of the rapidly decaying internal organs, and no attempt to draw off the water that makes up approximately three-quarters by weight of the human body. Beneath the bandages nature took her course and, when unwrapped, these prototype flexed mummies have decomposed into skeletons.

A major breakthrough came with the Old Kingdom realization that decomposition could be slowed by the prompt removal of the internal organs, followed by an intensive dehydration of the remaining soft tissue. Elongated rather than curled burials now became fashionable as the undertakers started to eviscerate their subjects via a slit in the abdomen before drying them in powdered natron. Natron, a naturally occurring drying agent (principally a mixture of sodium bicarbonate and sodium carbonate) with mild antiseptic properties, could be collected from the shores of the lakes in the Wadi en-Natrun. The entrails and lungs, which would be required by the deceased in the Afterlife, were at various times either stored in specially designed "canopic jars" or wrapped into bundles that could be incorporated within the mummy bandages. Magic would later ensure that the deceased was reunited with his or her organs.

Experimentation continued throughout the Old and Middle Kingdoms as the embalmers varied and refined their techniques until, by the New Kingdom, Egypt's morticians were confident in their ability to preserve a lifelike body. Unfortunately, the mysteries of mummification were never fully committed to papyrus. This is unlikely to be an accidental omission. Knowledge of the embalming rituals—a sacred as well as a practical rite— allowed the undertakers to exercise a powerful monopoly within their community. The vital secrets of the mortuary that would permit the dead to achieve eternal life were passed down from father to son.

Our best written description of mummification is that preserved by Herodotus in his *Histories, Book 2*, 86–88. Herodotus, fascinated by the whole curious process, obtained his information second-hand, long after the golden age of mummification had passed. Nevertheless, his account is extremely useful. He starts by telling us that the undertakers, like the undertakers of today, offered their clients a range of services: "These persons, when a corpse is brought to them, show the bereaved various models of bodies made in wood and painted to appear lifelike. One style is the most perfect . . . the second sort is inferior to the first while the third is cheapest of all. The embalmers explain all this, and then await their orders."

The best method was, naturally, the most costly; this is the technique detected in almost all of the dynastic mummies that have been unwrapped in modern times, and the technique that has proved most successful in experiments replicating mummification:

> . . . this is their procedure for the most perfect style of embalm-
> ing. First of all they draw out the brain through the nostrils
> using an iron hook. When they have extracted all that they can,
> they wash out the remnants with an infusion of drugs. Then,
> using a sharp obsidian stone, they make a cut along the flank.
> Through this they extract the whole contents of the abdomen.
> The abdomen is then cleaned, rinsed with palm wine and rinsed
> again with powdered spices but not frankincense, and stitched
> up. And when they have done this the body is placed in natron
> for seventy days. After the seventy days are over they wash the
> body and wrap it from head to toe in the finest linen bandages
> coated with resin which is used by the Egyptians as glue. . . .

The second, cheaper, method involved the injection of "cedar oil," possibly turpentine, to dissolve the internal organs which would then be
flushed out of the body via the rectum. Although a few mummies do lack
an evisceration scar, showing that they were either disembowelled by injection or mummified intact, this method is relatively rare:

> The embalmers fill their syringes with cedar oil which they in-
> ject into the abdomen. They do not cut the flesh or extract the
> internal organs, but introduce the oil through the anus which
> is then stopped up. Then they dry the body in natron for the
> prescribed number of days. After this they allow the oil which
> has been injected to escape. So great is its strength that it car-
> ries away all the internal organs in liquid state. The natron
> meanwhile has dissolved the flesh, so that there is nothing left
> but the skin and the bones.

The third, and cheapest, method was the least labour-intensive and
worthy of little description: "the undertakers clean out the abdomen with
a purge, mummify the corpse for seventy days, then give it back to be
taken away."

Herodotus, a Greek, concentrates on the practical aspects of mummification, giving little thought to the accompanying rituals. The Egyptians

themselves would have described the process very differently. Religion was the science of ancient Egypt; it explained how things worked and occasionally, as within the embalming workshop and the tomb, caused things to happen. Mummification was above all a religious rite—a rite which, if completed correctly, would ensure that the dead body could come back to life. The prescribed spells and incantations, the amulets and charms, were therefore as vital to the preservation of the corpse as the more obvious natron and bandages. The undertakers were priests rather than workmen, reciting spells and prayers and even donning ritual masks to act out the role of gods as they worked. Just one aspect of their ritual is known in some detail: Diodorus Siculus tells us that the "slitter," the man charged with cutting open the abdomen, would be ritually chased by the other undertakers who would feign anger and even throw stones in response to his assault on the corpse.

Herodotus' description, supplemented by additional details gleaned from the later classical authors such as Diodorus Siculus and Plutarch plus information obtained from modern unwrappings and discoveries of "embalmers' caches," allows us to reconstruct the three practical stages in the preparation of a traditional Egyptian mummy: the evisceration, the drying and the bandaging. Some experimental archaeologists have been able to test these techniques by mummifying animals and birds with a varying degree of success; only one team, Dr. Bob Brier of Long Island University, USA, and Ronald Wade, director of Maryland's State Anatomy Board, has actually mummified a human being.

Herodotus tells us of a special precaution for the bodies of certain women: "The wives of men of rank are not given to be embalmed immediately after death, nor indeed are any of the more beautiful or valued women. It is not until they have been dead for three or four days that they are taken to the embalmers. This is done to prevent indignities being practised upon them. It is said that once a case of this kind occurred, and that the man was detected by the information of his co-workers."

In some cases, the bodies of nubile women may well have been kept at home until they had lost their appeal. A few mummies, when unwrapped, have proved to be a mess of disarticulated bones, suggesting that decomposition was already well advanced when they were sent to the embalmers' workshop. An alternative suggestion of course is that they suffered some accident while undergoing treatment. Mishaps certainly did occur in the workshops, with the loss and subsequent restoration of digits, penises and even limbs a common occurrence. It is perhaps fortunate that those who paid for the mummification were unable to see beneath the neat bandages. Not even the royal embalmers got things right all the time. The 18th Dynasty Queen Ahmose-Nefertari undoubtedly suffered at the hands of the embalmers who, for no obvious reason, failed to halt her decay. The unfortunate queen smelt so strongly when unwrapped by Emile Brugsch in 1885 that she had to be temporarily re-buried until she had become more socially acceptable.

Other mummies show evidence of beetle and fly infestation, although whether this occurred before (indicating a delay) or during (indicating inefficiency) the embalming process it is difficult to say. Asru herself, although exceptionally well preserved, did not escape the omnipresent flies and her body yielded evidence of larval *Crysomyia*, an insect that lays its eggs on carrion.

Egypt is a hot country and so, under normal circumstances, her mortuary rituals were implemented as quickly as possible. Soon after death, before putrefaction and flies could start to cause problems, the deceased was taken to the Place of Purification, situated in the Redland away from the houses of the living. Here the body would be stripped and washed in a ritual act symbolizing rebirth. Next, the corpse would be transferred to the House of Mummification. As the body lay extended on a low table the removal of the decay-prone internal organs started. First the brain was extracted via the nose; a messy process that involved using a small chisel to break the nasal (ethmoid) bone and then dragging out fragments of tissue with an iron hook and a long-handled scoop. Any residue could be flushed out with liquid poured up the nose. As the liquid trickled out it would take the last cerebral fragments with it. Once empty, the head was filled with resin-soaked linen.

The abdomen was emptied by means of a cut on the left side made with a ritual "Ethiopian" or obsidian knife wielded by the "slitter." A subsequent cut upwards through the diaphragm allowed the removal of the lungs and the cleaning of the chest cavity. While the brain was discarded as useless, its function not understood, the organs removed from the chest and ab-domen—the liver, lungs, stomach and intestines—were preserved so that they might accompany the deceased into the Afterlife. Originally stored in canopic jars, at the time of Asru's death the undertakers were storing the desiccated and wrapped viscera within the mummy wrappings—either in-side the abdominal cavity, or associated with the feet and legs.

The heart and often the kidneys were left in the body. The kidneys were considered to be of little importance but the heart, the home of the intellect, would be needed to help the deceased when, in the judgement hall of Osiris, it would be weighed in the sacred scales. Hearts that were accidentally removed were sewn back, not always in the right place; the 19th Dynasty Seti I went to meet Osiris with his heart on the right side of his chest!

The emptied body was washed, packed with temporary stuffing mate-rial and then placed on a board, either sloping or provided with trestles to aid drainage, where it was covered with powdered natron. Here it would be left for forty days—although it seems likely that the sodden natron would be changed during this period—until it was thoroughly desiccated and ready to be emptied of its stuffing, washed, dried and coated with resin. The abdomen then received its permanent packing of resin-soaked linen, bags of sawdust or natron crystals before being stitched together, the wound magically healed by a gold eye of Horus amulet glued in position by yet more molten resin.

By the 21st Dynasty the embalmers had became expert in the art of packing and stuffing the shrunken bodies, via cuts in the skin and wadding in the cheeks, to give a lifelike appearance to the emaciated face and limbs. Any damaged or absent body parts could be restored at this stage; as we have already seen, displaced body parts were a common enough occur-rence and many mummies went to the Afterlife equipped with the false arms, legs, nipples and penises that would magically allow them to be-come whole. However, nothing could be done to save the eyeballs, which were pushed back into the socket and replaced by artificial eyes made from stones, painted linen or even onions. After the nostrils had been blocked and the tongue covered by a gold leaf, the mummy might be painted—yellow for women, red for men—and adorned with make-up and if necessary false hair. Finally the entire body was sealed in the molten resin that would protect against moisture and give the mummy a pleasant smell.

The bandaging of the desiccated corpse was a time-consuming, labour-intensive and highly symbolic task that magically converted the simple dead body into a mummy invested with the potential for resurrection and eternal life. To the Egyptians the bandaged body was a potential Osiris: an earthly form of the embalmed and bandaged god who ruled the underworld. They would not have recognized the word "mummy"; this is a relatively modern term derived from the Persian word for bitumen or pitch, *mummia*, a reference to the dark resin used to coat some of the later period bodies. Naturally, the bandaging was supervised by a priest who recited spells and incantations as he worked to a prescribed pattern.

The vast amounts of linen needed to wrap the corpse were provided by the bereaved family. While the wealthier members of society went to their Afterlife wrapped in many yards of fine sheets and specially purchased bandages, the less affluent made use of any spare cloth that they could get their hands on. We therefore find mummies bandaged in any cloth that could be torn into strips—old clothes, worn and patched sheets, soiled towels and even, in one case, an unwanted sail. The quantity of cloth used differed from mummy to mummy but it was always a great deal; an indication of the amount involved may be obtained from the 11th Dynasty mummy of the wealthy official Wah which, when unwrapped by the Metropolitan Museum of Art, New York, yielded an amazing 845 square metres (1010 square yards) of linen.

For its bandaging the body was laid on its back on a wooden trestle and covered by a yellow shroud. Wrapping patterns varied throughout the dynastic age, becoming increasingly elaborate with the passage of time. During the Third Intermediate Period, the time of Asru's mummification, it was usual for the wrapper to start by covering the head before individually wrapping the toes and fingers, then the feet and hands and finally the legs and arms. While the wrapped legs were then bandaged together from ankle to hip, the arms were bound along the torso with the palms either shielding the genitals or flat on the thighs. There was always a degree of variation in arm position, but it was only the royal mummies who regularly had their arms crossed over the chest. The bandagers then enveloped the body from head to foot, inserting amulets and charms where appropriate and using frequent applications of hot resin to glue the cloth in position. Finally the now-stiff mummy was dressed in one or more shrouds and the funerary mask or mummy board—an idealized likeness of the deceased—was fitted. After seventy days in the embalming house the mummy was finally ready for its coffin or coffins.

Wrapped and waiting for its funeral, the mummy was a being in suspense, neither living nor dead. Only the "Opening of the Mouth" ceremony, performed by a priest at the door of the tomb, could complete the spells started in the mortuary and bring the dead back to life. The Opening of the Mouth would restore the senses and bodily functions of the deceased.

On the chosen day the lengthy funeral procession would wend its way, with much wailing and dust thrown on heads, across the Nile and over the Redland to the open tomb. Here, at the doorway, the procession would halt as the mummy was taken out of its coffin and either held upright or propped on a pile of sand. While a lector-priest read out the relevant spells, a *sem*-priest touched the eyes, ears, mouth and nose of the mummy with a series of ritual implements including a forked knife, a chisel, an adze and a snake-headed rod. Offerings were made, including the foreleg of an ox slaughtered nearby, and the mummy was anointed with oils and ritually purified. The ceremony over, the mourners enjoyed a feast in the company of the now-restored deceased. Finally the coffined mummy was placed in the tomb alongside his or her grave goods. As the last guests departed, the tomb was swept in a ritual cleaning and the door sealed. With the body reanimated, the soul was now free to embark on its journey to the Field of Reeds.

The materials used and discarded in the embalming of the body could not be re-used on others. Nor, as they contained the essence of the deceased, could they simply be thrown away. Conscientious undertakers gathered up all the debris—the used natron, scraps of bandages, ointments and oils, vessels, tables and, of course, any bits that had fallen off or been extracted from the mummy—for burial either within the tomb or in a separate pit. The embalmers' cache associated with the mummification and burial of Tutankhamen, discovered by Theodore Davis in 1907, included not only the natron used in his embalming but the animal bones and floral collars that represent the remains of his funeral feast. The archaeological evidence suggests that this assemblage had originally been stored in the passageway of tomb KV 62, but had been moved by the priests who restored the tomb and blocked its entrance with limestone chips following the first robbery.

So well established was the Osirian way of death that the Greeks and Romans who settled in Egypt at the end of the dynastic era abandoned their own funerary traditions and adopted mummification for their own dead. Eventually, however, the advent of Christianity heralded the end of mummification. The journey to the Field of Reeds was no longer undertaken, and Egypt's Coptic dead would cast off their earthly bodies to rise to heaven. In consequence they were interred intact, unembalmed and unadorned.

Over thirty centuries of mummification had left many thousands of preserved bodies stored in Egypt's tombs and graves. As the centuries passed this valuable natural resource was to be exploited in many ingenious ways. Mummies were ground up for medicine, for paint and for paper manufacture; they were burned as fuel, stripped and robbed of their amulets, and sold to the ever increasing numbers of tourists who required a gruesome souvenir to horrify their stay-at-home friends. From 1698 onwards, the time that the French Consul in Cairo performed the first public unwrapping of a mummy, "unrollings" were a popular entertainment with interested observers jostling for positions around the autopsy table. Although there were some who took this work seriously—the surgeon Thomas Joseph Pettigrew (1791–1864), for example, published the results of his many public unrollings—most did not. Indeed, given the limited medical techniques available to these early pathologists, it is not surprising that the potential of the mummies as unique sources of information was overlooked. As the anatomist Grafton Elliot Smith expressed it in *The Royal Mummies*:

> In discussing the technique of mummification and the customs associated with it one has to deal with subjects that may possibly give rise to offence, on the ground that it is not showing due respect to the memories of the powerful rulers of Ancient Egypt

to display their naked remains, and use them as material for anthropological investigations. In fact a good deal of comment has been made in the past in reference to the so-called "sacrilege," on the part of modern archaeologists, in opening royal tombs and removing and unwrapping the mummies.

Gradually there came a growing awareness that it might not be suitable to treat the unveiling of the dead—albeit the very ancient dead—as an entertaining spectacle. Public unrollings slowly ceased, although mummies continued to be exposed in museums and laboratories, often in front of an invited audience. There has been one notable exception to this rule. When, in 1981, the mummy of Horemkenesi was unwrapped in the Department of Anatomy, Bristol University, the operation was filmed and relayed to an audience watching from the entrance hall of the City Museum.

When the Deir el-Bahari mummies were unrolled in Cairo in the late nineteenth century, two major assumptions were made: no one questioned that almost all of the royal mummies should be unwrapped; and no one queried the fact that the operation was being performed by an Egyptologist rather than by a doctor or anatomist. The emphasis was still very much on discovering as quickly as possible what lay below the bandages. This approach was to undergo rapid change over the next hundred years as the painstaking work of the anatomists Grafton Elliot Smith and Douglas Derry showed exactly how much information a skilfully analysed mummy could reveal. Smith, for one, felt that Egypt's mummies could be as informative as her historical texts: "Having these valuable historical 'documents' in our possession it is surely our duty to read them as fully and as carefully as possible."

The development of X-ray analysis in 1895 had been quickly followed by the X-raying of the first mummies—a child and a cat—in 1896. Although it was to take several decades for this to become a universally available and affordable technique, Egyptologists recognized that they at last had a non-destructive means of peering below the mummy bandages. Indeed, it was even possible to X-ray a mummy without removing it from its coffin. The results of this work were occasionally surprising; the Lady Teshat for example, outwardly perfect, was found to have been mummified with an extra head, while a Graeco-Roman "child" mummy in Liverpool University Museum was entirely composed of cat bones!

Today, as further advances in medical science provide a range of useful analytical techniques, unwrapping a mummy is seen as the ultimate rescue operation, only to be undertaken if the existence of the mummy is already threatened by decomposition or infestation. There have been only four official unrollings of mummies in the British Isles in the past hundred years: three at Manchester University, and one under the supervision of Bristol Museum.

CHAPTER ELEVEN

Who?
Investigating Asru

When I first saw Asru I thought that she looked in fact quite well preserved. Obviously I looked for evidence of disease externally, but I didn't really see anything. The only thing I did notice was that she was on the thin side and it made one wonder if she might well have been suffering from diseases that could have caused her to have lost weight.

Histo-pathologist Dr Edmund Tapp

MANCHESTER MUSEUM IS A PART OF MANCHESTER UNIVERSITY, WHICH HAS a strong tradition of medical and dental studies. The museum, taking full advantage of its close links with the medical faculties and local hospitals, has developed a formidable expertise in mummy studies. Its first multidisciplinary investigation occurred in 1907, when the Egyptologist Margaret Murray conducted a detailed examination, including unwrapping and dissection, of the remains of Nakhtankh and Khnumnakht, two 12th

Dynasty mummies more popularly known as the "Two Brothers." The results of this work were published in 1910 as *The Tomb of the Two Brothers*. Tissue samples taken from these early unwrappings were preserved and re-examined during the 1970s by the Manchester Museum Mummy Project, a programme instigated by Rosalie David, Curator of Egyptology. The aim was to facilitate the study of all the museum's mummies and mummified body parts, using a wide range of current scientific techniques.

One of the stated aims of the Manchester Museum Mummy Project was to establish a methodology for the examination of ancient Egyptian human remains, which other institutions could subsequently follow and adapt for the study of their own collections. As part of this work, it was decided to perform an autopsy on one of the museum's mummies. In June 1975 a specialized team was assembled in the university medical school to unwrap Mummy 1770, an anonymous Graeco-Roman of obscure origins.

Mummy 1770 proved to be a young girl, approximately thirteen years of age at death. The girl was not in good condition. Indeed, at the time of her mummification, she had been so badly damaged that the embalmers could not even be certain of her gender. She had therefore gone to meet Osiris provided not only with an artificial leg and two artificial feet dressed in elaborately decorated slippers, but with the gilded nipples and a false penis that would enable her to be reborn as either a woman or a man. The story behind the young girl's death remains obscure; had she fallen into the Nile and been partially eaten by a crocodile? Had she perhaps been withheld from the embalming house until she literally fell apart? Or was she simply the unfortunate result of mortuary negligence? Radiocarbon dating was later to suggest that she was a Third Intermediate Period girl who had for some reason been rewrapped a thousand years after her first mummification.

The multi-disciplinary approach developed for the unwrapping of Mummy 1770 was now to be followed and developed for the medical investigation of Asru. Asru, apart from her extreme thinness, showed no immediate evidence of sickness and no obvious cause of death. The study was therefore concerned to establish whether or not her mummy held hidden evidence of diseases prevalent among the upper classes of Third Intermediate Period Egypt.

Unfortunately, Asru's already unwrapped state meant that textile analysis, an important part of the work on Mummy 1770, could not be included in the study. Modern mummy projects pay a great deal of attention to the mummy wrappings which earlier investigators cheerfully discarded; it is now recognized that careful unwrapping can provide details not only of the bandaging techniques and of the cloth itself but of local conditions at the time of embalming. Many mummies have been found to have diagnostic sediments, beetles and fly larvae incorporated within their wrappings and fixed within their resin. The sand and sediments discovered on the body of Ramesses II suggest, for example, that this particular king could not have been embalmed on the banks of the Nile at Thebes.

Asru was to undergo a battery of medical tests. She had already been X-rayed as part of the 1970s Mummy Project. Her re-examined radiographs provided clear evidence that Asru was an elderly lady. Indeed, by Egyptian standards she was positively ancient; throughout the dynastic age anyone over the age of forty-five was considered to have exceeded their natural span. Degenerative arthritis, a persistent ancient Egyptian complaint, is commonly found in mummies of all social classes over the age of thirty-five. Asru was no exception. Her fingers revealed unmistakable osteoarthritic, or degenerative arthritic, changes to the joints. This, combined with evidence of calcification in the aorta and the bronchi and in the lower legs and feet, and arthritis in the knee, suggests that Asru was probably older than fifty but lacking the changes that we might expect to find in a person over seventy years of age.

The X-ray lateral view of Asru's lower spine indicated that she had at some stage suffered a lumbar vertebral fracture. As there were signs of subsequent new bone formation, this trauma must have occurred some years before Asru's death. Increased calcification in the lower back region may well have been connected with the old injury which, by causing pressure on the nerve roots from the spinal cord, probably caused Asru to experience a sciatica-like pain down her left leg.

Active people, those who expose the joints to excessive wear and tear, may well develop arthritis earlier than the inactive. We know that Asru was a chantress or singer and that, as part of her temple duties, she may also have been required to dance or even play a musical instrument. It is not

clear how vigorous these activities would have been but, if Asru was expected to play an instrument such as the harp on a regular basis, her musical skills may have contributed towards the damage seen in her finger
joints. Playing the harp may, however, have been a problem in Asru's later
years; further examination of her hands revealed that infection or septic
arthritis in her left hand had destroyed the joint of the third digit.

A clue to the extent of Asru's temple duties is provided by the well-
preserved skin of her hands and feet. Asru's finger- and toe-prints had already been taken by Detective Chief Inspector A. Fletcher of the Greater
Manchester Police. This was a delicate operation. Under normal circumstances fingerprints are recorded by rolling one digit at a time over an
inkpad and then making an impression on paper. However, the rigidity of
Asru's hands, and the fragile nature of her skin, ruled out this technique.
Instead, Asru's prints were first captured in dental modelling compound
and then cast in acrylic. The resulting acrylic finger- and toe-tips proved
robust enough to be inked and printed in the usual way.

Asru's fingertips suggested to the police experts that she was a lady in
her late forties (something of an underestimate), unaccustomed to hard
manual work and with fingertips that showed little evidence of prolonged
harp playing. Similarly, her feet did not exhibit the flattening and wear that
might have been expected from a barefoot dancer, indicating that Asru's
temple duties may well have been confined to singing.

A series of X-rays allowed a thorough dental examination of Asru's teeth
and jaw. Her surviving front teeth showed evidence of a substantial over-
bite, with her upper incisors completely overlapping the lower ones. Her
back teeth—many of which were missing, lost before death—revealed
that Asru must have suffered from prolonged and painful bouts of
toothache. There was evidence of serious infection in her jaw, with some
destruction of bone around the roots of the teeth presumably caused by
abscesses. The remaining teeth showed little sign of caries but had been
flattened, presenting the square appearance characteristic of the severe attrition found in many dynastic mummies. As we have already seen from
our consideration of earlier Egyptian remains, the inadvertent inclusion
of grit (from the grinding stones used in the manufacture of bread) and
wind-borne sand within the diet slowly but surely wore down not only

the cusps of the teeth, but the body of them as well. In the most severe cases this could lead to the exposure of the pulp chamber and the development of abscesses.

Toothache was accepted as an inevitable, incurable and occasionally fatal feature of pharaonic old age. Dentistry was at best basic, a religious art rather than a science, and pain control was minimal. The New Kingdom Ebers Medical Papyrus suggests some recipes:

> The beginning of remedies to fasten a tooth: powdered ammi, yellow ochre and honey are mixed together and the tooth is filled therewith . . . .

> To expel growth of purulency in the gums: sycamore fruit, beans, honey, malachite and yellow ochre are ground and applied to the tooth.

> To treat a tooth which is eaten away where the gums begin: cumin, frankincense and carob pulp are powdered and applied to the tooth.

The next investigation of Asru's body involved, for the first time, a CAT- or CT- scan. CAT (Computed Axial Tomography) analysis is a more sophisticated form of X-ray analysis, whereby the rays are recorded not on film but by a highly sensitive scintillation or ionization detector linked to a computer. The X-ray tube and the detector are free to rotate around the patient, allowing a series of thin sections or slices to be taken through the body. The computer is then able to reconstruct the sections in any plane, creating a three-dimensional image of the patient. On a CAT-scan it is possible to see not only the bone, air and fat revealed by conventional X-ray techniques, but also the soft tissue structures.

The introduction of CAT-scans in the early 1970s revolutionized modern medical diagnosis, as it was for the first time possible to examine the living skull without using a contrast medium to see the hollows and vessels within the brain. Egyptologists have found this a very useful method of examining mummies because it is non-invasive, it does not require the presence of water in the tissue (the desiccation of the mummies inhibits the use of magnetic resonance imaging or MRI) and, by revealing the soft tissue, it allows the location of any organs or packets of preserved organs within the body cavity. The CT work on Asru's head, for example, disclosed the presence of remnants of brain tissue within her skull cavity which conventional X-ray analysis had been unable to detect.

Using information derived from the CAT-scans, a solid polymer replica of Asru's skull was cut by laser. This skull was to be used as the basis of a facial reconstruction performed by expert Caroline Wilkinson of Manchester University. Facial reconstruction, the modelling of clay muscle and skin on to the skull-base, is a relatively modern technique that has been developed to bring the dead back to some semblance of life. The method depends upon the fact that the size, shape and features of the human head and face are largely determined by the shape of the skull and the teeth. Using an internationally recognized system of measurements devised by Kollmann and Buchly in 1898, it is possible to calculate the expected depth of the soft tissue at twenty-three defined points on the face. The skin on the upper forehead, for example, is expected to be some 3.56 millimetres thick, that in the middle of the eyebrow 3.65 millimetres. The expert therefore proceeds by fixing a series of measured pegs into the model skull to indicate skin thickness at the defined points, and then building up the clay around the pegs. The modelling of the cartilaginous nose can present a challenge; width can be determined by the width of the nasal cavity but the ultimate shape and profile will always include some guesswork.

Wrinkles and blemishes cannot, of course, be reconstructed with any degree of accuracy. It is therefore unlikely that an exact likeness to the deceased will ever be obtained. Nevertheless, despite this obvious limitation, modern police reconstructions have proved the accuracy of the technique by helping with the identification of badly decomposed or otherwise damaged bodies. As a further test of the method, an experiment was conducted in the Department of Anatomy, Manchester University. Three bodies, due to be dissected by medical students, were photographed. After dissection the skulls were cast and reconstructed by experts who had not been shown the original photographs. Unfortunately one set of photographs had gone missing, but the remaining male and female reconstructions proved the general accuracy of the method, with only the reconstruction of the nose causing a problem.

Asru's mummified head, although very well preserved for her age, is both withered and distorted, her face an unnatural colour and lacking both eyeballs and nose. Nakhtankh, Khnumnakht and Mummy 1770 had already been reconstructed. Now the experts wanted to see how Asru might have looked shortly before her death.

Reconstructed, painted and bewigged, Asru was revealed as an elderly lady with high cheekbones, a small pointed chin and problem teeth causing sunken cheeks and a protruding upper lip. Her eyes were deep-set, in contrast to her long, wide nose and her large ears with pronounced lobes which had been modelled on the ears on Asru's anthropoid coffin. Asru had a slightly elongated, but by no means deformed, head.

The CAT-scan had confirmed that there were traces of lung and bladder tissue within the mummy that could be further examined and biopsied by endoscopy. Endoscopy, the insertion of a narrow tube equipped with a viewing camera into the body, has been used in the examination of living patients for many years. In mummies the obvious places to insert the tube, the mouth and the anus, are often blocked so, as in Asru's case, it may be necessary to make a small hole in the wall of the chest. The tissue samples thus obtained need to be rehydrated and cut into thin sections before they can be examined by microscope.

Asru's lung tissue showed evidence of an environmentally determined and potentially fatal disease. Sand pneumoconiosis, an affliction associated with the inhalation of small wind-borne sand particles, is very common in dynastic mummies and is still found among present-day nomadic populations. The disease scars the lungs, with the resulting loss of respiratory function leading to breathlessness and bouts of coughing. Eventually it may affect the circulation, causing heart failure. Asru's lung tissue revealed the typical scarring plus minute particles of sand. Similar scarring has been found in the other Manchester mummies, including the recently analysed lung tissue taken from Nakhtankh some sixty years earlier and sensibly preserved in a glass jar by Margaret Murray. It seems that this unfortunate "Brother" had suffered from a combination of sand pneumoconiosis, pleurisy and pericarditis. Anthracosis, a disease caused by carbon rather than sand inhalation, and presumably the result of sitting in enclosed smoky environments, has been identified in several autopsied mummies.

The River Nile, the vital flowing vein that allowed Egypt to flourish in an otherwise arid desert zone, was acknowledged and even worshipped as the bringer of life. Without the Nile there could be no Egypt: the Egyptians exploited their river to the full as a highway, a source of food and drink, a means of irrigation and recreation, a laundry, a bath and a sewer. Unfortunately, the Nile also brought sickness to the masses. The damp soil, slow-moving canals and stagnant pools at the water's edge provided a fertile breeding ground for a variety of parasitic worms plus the mosquitoes that carry malaria. Most Egyptians, unaware of the dangers in their river, would have had fairly regular contact with stagnant water. Some, fishermen and laundrymen to name the most obvious, would have spent much of their working day with their feet in the Nile.

All too often, the evidence of parasitic infestation disappears with the death and decomposition of the host, although under unusual circumstances the evidence may survive. This most commonly occurs when the parasite dies within living tissue, and calcification occurs to preserve its form. X-ray examination of Mummy 1770, for example, showed the presence of a calcified male Guinea worm in her abdominal wall. Mummy 1770 had been lucky; while the male Guinea worm develops to only a few centimetres in length before fertilizing the female and dying, the female worm may grow to an astonishing 1 metre (3 feet) within the leg or foot of the host.

The team already knew that Asru had suffered from at least two parasitic infections, and Asru herself may have recognized that her stools included worms. In 1976, as part of the Mummy Project, Asru's preserved intestines had been rehydrated and examined. This work had revealed the presence of the larval form of the *Nematode strongyloides* worm in her intestinal wall. *Strongyloides* infection, a common problem in ancient Egypt, still persists in tropical and sub-tropical Africa and India where it may be contracted by walking barefoot through water, mud or soil contaminated with the immature worm. The worm penetrates the skin of the feet or hands to reach the blood vessels. This allows the worm to travel around its human host, first to the heart, next to the lungs and then up the windpipe to the throat where the worms are swallowed and descend to the intestine. Here the immature forms develop into adults, causing irritation which leads to bloody diarrhoea and maybe anaemia. Eggs are laid in the intestine and, as the eggs are excreted with the stools, the cycle starts again.

Now Asru's newly discovered fragments of bladder tissue, sectioned and stained, showed clear microscopic evidence of schistosomiasis or bilharzia infestation. Bilharzia has been found in mummies of all ages, and it remains a major health hazard in the modern Nile Valley. The retention of bilharzia eggs within the human host causes serious medical problems. The eggs are spiked and, as they hook into the body tissue, can cause serious tears. Once this damage has been done fibrosis will occur around the eggs. This damages the tissue even more, and may eventually lead to cancer.

Both ancient and modern bilharzia infection can be identified by testing for the presence of antibodies. This suggests that over thousands of years the organism has remained fundamentally unchanged. The investigation of the ancient bilharzia flukes is therefore a matter of interest to specialists, including cancer specialists, working with more modern forms of the parasite. It is hoped that the comparison and cross-referencing of the worms identified in the mummies with the modern worms may eventually be of help in determining those parts of their genetic code that promote the development of cancer.

The parasitic cycle of the bilharzia fluke is well understood. Bilharzia worms lay their eggs in the human host; these enter the bladder or the intestine via the bloodstream and are released into fresh water in urine or faeces. Once the eggs are in the water they hatch and then the larvae burrow into the intermediate secondary host, a water snail. Here the fluke changes form and leaves the snail to return to the water. Re-entering a human host, usually by burrowing into the feet, the fluke moves upwards to the liver or the bladder where it mates and produces eggs which continue its life-cycle. Asru appears to have contracted *Schistosoma haematobium*, the species that lays its eggs in the bladder. This causes tissue damage that leads to blood in the urine, often the first sign that someone has been infected. Eventually calcification of the bladder will occur, with fluid retention leading to swelling of the stomach, pain, exhaustion and sickness.

Asru had contracted a third parasitic worm. The X-ray examination of her chest area had disclosed a shadow, originally thought to be connected with the heart. Subsequent endoscopic examination revealed this to be a hydatid cyst, possibly measuring up to twenty centimetres (eight inches) in diameter, holding the immature form of the dog tapeworm *Echinococcus granulosus*. Dog tapeworm usually exploits sheep as its intermediate host, but it has been found in other mummies who had presumably been in contact with contaminated dog faeces. However, pork tapeworm is the tapeworm more commonly recovered from mummies, suggesting that undercooked pork formed an important part of the dynastic diet.

The dog tapeworm partially develops in the intestine and then, by burrowing its way through the intestinal wall, makes its way to the liver, the kidney, the lungs or the brain. Here the tapeworm develops into a fluid-filled cyst. The location of the cyst is crucial to the survival of the patient. A cyst in the brain can kill quite rapidly: the Manchester mummy-head 22940 apparently died of a brain cyst that included several tapeworm heads. A cyst like Asru's, lodged in the more spacious lungs, would eventually cause breathlessness and perhaps pleurisy. Perhaps she tried a remedy to kill tapeworm suggested by the Ebers Medical Papyrus: "colocynth, turpentine, grease, red natron, and gall of ox are shaped into cake and eaten in one day...."

The evidence revealed by the medical examination of Asru's mummified body forces us to rethink the idealized images of carefree, hygienic daily life presented by Egypt's tomb walls. Asru was born a member of the privileged upper classes but this offered her little protection against the unseen hazards of her natural environment. As she entered old age, Asru's quality of life was blighted and eventually ended by a series of painful and debilitating conditions including anaemia, diarrhoea, toothache, arthritis, leg pain, coughing and breathlessness. Egypt's doctors, although the best in the ancient world, were denied the diagnostic techniques and the medical understanding that have allowed us to identify Asru's various ailments. They could do nothing to cure her afflictions and could merely attempt to treat the observable symptoms. As Rosalie David has summarized:

Asru was from an upper-class background, and maybe this contributed to her fairly lengthy life because she probably had the best diet available and a relatively relaxed lifestyle. She would not have been engaged in housework, there would have been servants in the house, and so on. But we also know from this evidence that she had a painful life with diseases that would have brought her physical difficulties. And so you can get a very rounded picture of the kind of world she lived in.

CHAPTER TWELVE

How?
Scents
and Sexuality

It may well be that Asru took some medication for her various
illnesses, particularly in response to the pain of her arthritis.

Hospital anaesthetist David Counsell

ASRU'S INFESTED BODY, WHICH WE MIGHT EXPECT TO BE TYPICAL FOR A
woman of her time, age and class, suggests that she would have experienced gradually increasing pain and discomfort as her long life progressed.
It therefore seems reasonable to assume that she would have made good
use of any painkillers available to her.

The nature and extent of dynastic drug use, for both medicinal and
recreational purposes, is a matter of intense academic debate. Archaeological, textual and pictoral evidence shows that the Egyptians used alco-
hol, drinking copious quantities of beer and wine, and we can see from
the medical papyri that they prepared medicines that they hoped would

be effective against a wide range of ills. Although there is no formal record of them enjoying any form of recreational drug, some experts have suggested that drugs may indeed have been used to enhance both banquets and temple rituals. The Manchester team therefore decided to test Asru's tissue and hair in order to expand understanding of this hidden aspect of pharaonic society.

The testing of mummy tissue for drugs is a relatively new development, and one that has so far yielded some puzzling results. The mummy of Ramesses II, for example, has given evidence of nicotine. Tobacco is a New World plant introduced to the Old World more than fifteen centuries after the end of the dynastic age; there is no other evidence, either written or archaeological, to support its use or even its presence in Ramesside Egypt. It therefore seems unlikely that Ramesses smoked tobacco and, accepting the accuracy of the test results, we must conclude that Ramesses has in some way been contaminated by the smoking archaeologists who have had care of his body for the past century.

More controversial still are the findings of the German scientist Svelta Balabonova, that seven mummies, ranging in date from the Third Intermediate to the Roman Periods, hold traces of cannabis, cocaine and once again nicotine. The cannabis is not surprising: hemp was grown in Egypt and is known to have been used in the manufacture of medicinal drugs. However, coca is also an American plant. It seems unlikely that the mummies have been contaminated by cocaine-sprinkling archaeologists, and so we are forced to conclude that either there has been a misidentification, or that the accepted history of both nicotine and coca is incorrect.

One drug that has not yet been identified in mummy tissue is morphine, or opium. Opium, the dried juice of the opium poppy (*Papaver somniferum L.*), has sedative, painkilling and euphoric properties much appreciated by mankind. We know that the opium poppy was being grown in Anatolia by 2000 BCE. However, the question of the Egyptian use, or non-use, of opium is hotly debated. The medical papyri mention the drug *spn*, a word that linguists have tentatively translated as "poppy." *Spn* appears to have possessed narcotic effects invaluable to fraught mothers, as the Ebers Medical Papyrus suggests: "Remedy to expel crying in a child: *spn* seeds and fly's dirt taken from the wall are mixed together, strained and taken for four days. The child will cease crying immediately."

Some Egyptologists maintain that opium was in widespread use in Egypt from the Second Intermediate Period onwards. This controversial theory, first put forward by Egyptologist Robert Merrillees in 1962, is supported not by finds or written descriptions of opium and opium use, but by a series of distinctive Cypriot pottery juglets, shaped like inverted poppy heads and recovered from Egypt. For many, these juglets offer clear evidence of an international drugs trade, with opium being grown in Anatolia and imported into Egypt, dissolved in water or wine, by Cypriot merchants. Thus opium would form part of the Late Bronze Age network that saw luxury goods circulating in an anti-clockwise direction around the eastern Mediterranean.

The fact that the juglets cease to appear in post 18th-Dynasty contexts has been plausibly explained by the fact that the Egyptians had themselves started to cultivate the poppy, and therefore no longer imported opium, around this date. Others have remained unconvinced. While they would agree that the juglets must have been designed to hold luxury goods, they would argue that it cannot be assumed, merely on the basis of their shape, that they originally held opium.

The best way to test the opium theory is to analyse any residue in the surviving juglets, looking for traces of opium alkaloids (the most important of which are morphine, codeine and thebaine) or the remains of their degraded and oxidized products. However, the interpretation of the results thus obtained requires a degree of caution. While the presence of opium within a juglet may be taken as conclusive proof that that juglet once held opium, it cannot be assumed that opium was the juglet's original content. Similarly, the absence of opium may simply indicate that a particular juglet, considered a precious item in its own right, had been emptied, cleaned and re-used.

In recent years the residue of a series of juglets has been submitted for analysis by different experts. While most have yielded negative results, a few have apparently confirmed the presence of opium alkaloids—although some of the published positive results have subsequently been challenged. The residue in the juglets tested by the Manchester team, using the most detailed and sophisticated analytical techniques available, gave negative results. However, at least one juglet, part of the collection of the Wurzburg University Museum (inventory number A39), has yielded undisputed, double-tested evidence of morphine. Unfortunately, the history and precise provenance of this juglet is not known, so that there is always a danger of secondary contamination. To assume from this one positive result that all the negative-testing juglets originally held opium is a logical but somewhat bold step. It perhaps seems prudent to reach a verdict of not proven on the widespread use of opium in post-Second Intermediate Period Egypt.

Samples of Asru's scalp, and tissue samples retrieved by endoscopy, were tested for drugs by members of the Manchester team: analytical chemist Vic Garner and hospital anaesthetist David Counsell. It was hoped that the tissue might yield evidence of any drugs taken immediately before Asru's death, possibly painkillers, while a hair sample might include drugs taken over a longer period for either medicinal or recreational purposes. Garner and Counsell employed a variety of techniques to search for a range of drugs including opium alkaloids (particularly morphine), cannabinoids and the alkaloids that some Egyptologists believed might be found in the blue lotus flower. However, all these tests proved negative. While there were many compounds found within Asru's tissue there was no trace of any narcotic, and no evidence that Asru had taken any recognized form of drug.

Asru's scalp with only a residual growth of hair had to provide the sample as her head had been shaved—shaven heads were not unusual in her society. The Egyptians placed great importance on personal hygiene and the appearance of total cleanliness which, on their tomb walls, was emphasized by their unblemished white clothing. Fashions varied from age to age but the upper classes had a tendency to remove all visible hair, using a mixture of shaving, plucking and a form of waxing involving an unsavoury compound of crushed bird bone and fly dirt. The bald head would then, on formal occasions, be covered by an elaborately dressed wig of human hair.

The inclusion of razors and tweezers among both male and female grave goods confirms that depilation was considered an essential element of the toilette. Whether this was a beautifying, a medical or even a religious ritual, as Herodotus (*Histories, Book 2*: 367) suggests, is not clear; probably, as with so many aspects of Egyptian life, it had a mixed purpose: "In other countries the priests have long hair; in Egypt their heads are shaven. Elsewhere it is customary, in mourning, for near relations to cut their hair close; the Egyptians, who wear no hair at any other time, when they lose a relative let their beards and head hair grow long. . . . The priests shave the whole body every other day, that no lice or any other impure thing may stick to them when they are serving the gods."

The hair-free body would then be washed—although not with soap, which was unknown—and deodorant manufactured from incense and porridge would be applied under the arms. Finally eyeliner was applied by both men and women. Again, this was a combination of vanity and practicality as the Egyptians believed that their eye makeup would protect against disease. Sore and inflamed eyes, made worse by the glaring sunlight and the wind-borne sand, were a constant problem throughout the dynastic age. While some, believing their blindness to be a punishment inflicted by the gods, prayed for a cure, the medical profession offered alternative although scarcely more practical advice—as here, from the Ebers Medical Papyrus:

> For night blindness in the eyes: ox liver, roasted and ground, is given. This is really excellent!

> To expel blindness in the eyes by means of a pellet: dry myrrh is ground with the viscous fluid of fermented drink and applied to the eyelids.

> To improve the sight: cream and the breast-milk of a woman who has borne a male child are mixed together and dropped in the eye.

Modern analysis of ancient eyeliner residue taken from cosmetic pots housed in the Louvre Museum, Paris, has confirmed that lead—believed by many to heal sore eyes—was deliberately incorporated into the eye makeup, making it a therapeutic compound.

Any lingering body odour could be masked by the use of a mouthwash and a generous application of scent. Smells, beautiful and otherwise, played an inescapable role in Egyptian daily life. Unfortunately this is one aspect of dynastic society that is difficult for modern observers to appreciate, although Victor Loret came close when, in 1898, he breached the sealed doorway to the tomb of Tuthmosis III in the Valley of the Kings. Loret was stopped in his tracks by the heat and overpowering smell emanating from the tomb; the smell was that of scented cedarwood mingled with the other tomb perfumes. More disastrously, the writer Amelia B. Edwards, a contemporary visitor to Luxor who published her adventures in *A Thousand Miles up the Nile*, tells of the unfortunate fate that awaited a fragranced mummy purchased by two fellow travellers: "They bought both mummy and papyrus at an enormous price; and then, unable to bear the perfume of their ancient Egyptian, drowned the dear departed at the end of a week."

It is to be hoped that the drowned Egyptian was not one of the missing royal mummies stolen from the Deir el-Bahari cache!

Many of Egypt's odours must have been distinctly unpleasant. The people lived in close proximity both to each other and to their livestock. Sanitation was minimal, washing facilities few and far between, and the weather was almost always hot. Most houses had no toilet facilities; their residents simply made use of the nearby fields. Those homes that did possess a toilet had a simple box-like affair enclosing a pottery vessel which, after use, was covered with a layer of sand scooped from a handily placed pot. Eventually, as the toilet grew full, it was emptied away from the house. It is not surprising that even an upper-class lady like Asru contracted parasitic infestations indicative of low hygiene and contact with human and animal faeces.

Perfumes and scented fats were an important element in the Egyptian toilette. Scent was extracted from flowers and fragrant woods by soaking in oil. The perfumed oil would then be diluted, fixed with gum or resin and stored in elegant flasks. *Kyphie*, an oil-free perfume manufactured from wine, raisins, frankincense and herbs, was both burned in temples and added to wine. The recipe for *kyphie* was considered so valuable that it was included on the walls of the Graeco-Roman temples at Philae and at Edfu, where there was a little room dedicated to the production of perfume fit for the gods. Incense, too, played a role both in temple ritual and domestic hygiene where fumigation both covered unpleasant smells and, by releasing carbolic acid, killed fleas, mice and other unwanted house guests.

As in our own society, scent had a strong link with sexuality and pleasure. We have already seen how, when Queen Ahmose, mother-to-be of Queen Hatchepsut, was visited by the amorous god Amen "the palace was flooded with the god's fragrance, and all his perfumes were as from Punt [the faraway land of the incense trees] . . . ." The curious pale cones that Egyptian revellers invariably wear on their heads are cones of scented fat. Traditionally it has been assumed that these cones would, in the heat of the party, melt and trickle down the head in a refreshing perfumed stream. However, considering the obvious practical difficulties in manufacturing a substance that would melt satisfactorily at just above normal room temperature, it may perhaps be wiser to interpret these cones as symbols of scentedness; the informed observer would realize, when a cone was being worn, that the wearer was exquisitely perfumed.

Given this obvious love of flower-based perfume, it is not surprising to find beautiful scented flowers figuring prominently in tomb and temple scenes. Flowers were offered to the gods in truly impressive quantities: we know that in just under three years the 20th Dynasty king Ramesses III presented almost two million bouquets plus many assorted wreaths and single blossoms to the Karnak temple of Amen. Flowers also played an important role in funerary ritual where they were both worn by mourners and included in the sealed tombs. Tutankhamen's intact burial confirms that kings were buried with a series of floral tributes; the boy king himself had a magnificent beaded collar, incorporating berries, leaves, cornflower heads and blue lotus petals, resting on his innermost golden coffin.

Egypt was not over-endowed with wild flowers. Her natural vegetation, confined to the fertile strip fringing the Nile and the Nile Delta, consisted of scrubland with a predominance of grasses and reeds in the damper areas. Private gardens were considered a great luxury. Here the shaded, artificially watered gardens of the wealthy were planted with neat rows of trees and flowerbeds including poppies, cornflowers and mandrake. Their ornamental ponds housed papyrus and the white and blue lotus. Any or all of these flowers might be used in composite bouquets, but it was the blue lotus, a form of water lily, which played the most prominent role in Egyptian life and ritual. An Egyptian lover, wishing to impress the beloved whose "fingers are like lotus buds," would press his suit not with roses but with lotus blossoms.

The symbolic role of the lotus in Egyptian religion is well understood. The white lotus (*Nymphaea lotus L.*) and the blue lotus (*Nymphaea caerulea*) represented life itself. One of the Egyptian creation myths tells how the sun god Re appeared as a child floating on the primeval waters in a lotus. The lotus is also the emblem of the Memphite god Nefertum, son of Ptah and Sekhmet, and Nefertum too may be depicted emerging from a lotus flower. It is therefore not surprising to find this rejuvenating flower included time and time again within temples and tombs. However, was the lotus appreciated simply because of its beauty, its scent and its association with creation, or did it have a more direct role to play in ancient rituals, perhaps being consumed or sniffed as a mind-altering drug?

Danish Egyptologist Lise Manniche believes that this might have been the case. Translating a previously obscure inscription found in the Graeco-Roman temple of Horus at Edfu, she cites a section where the king talks to the god about the blue lotus: "When you look at its brilliance your eyes become imbued with dynamic force. When you breathe in your nostrils dilate."

Manniche has suggested that this might be an accurate description of a person sniffing a hallucinogenic substance. David Counsell and Vic Garner were not convinced. Although they recognized that the blue lotus had a pleasant smell, somewhat reminiscent of banana, they felt that it would be very unlikely that its alkaloid could be appreciated by simple sniffing. As other Egyptologists had also, working independently, suggested that the ubiquitous blue lotus might have been appreciated for its narcotic powers, Garner and Counsell decided to put this theory to the test.

Unfortunately the blue lotus, so common in dynastic Egypt, is now rare. Eventually, having obtained samples from Cairo, from Tel Aviv and from a British botanical garden where the lotus had been raised in controlled conditions similar to those found in Egypt, the team was able to test for narcotics using techniques of mass spectrometry.

Tomb and temple scenes indicate two distinct ways in which the blue lotus might have been consumed: it might have been added to wine and drunk, or it might have been inhaled. Samples for analysis were therefore obtained by soaking the lotus in methanol (a wine substitute) to make a lotus-solution, and by extracting air from the air-space immediately above the flower to capture its perfume. In neither case was any trace of alkaloid found. As David Counsell has summarized: "I think that our findings both from the head space and from the more detailed analysis of the flower itself have proven that there are no alkaloids in the flower that could produce any narcotic effect. So I think that we have to kick into touch the narcotic possibilities of the blue lotus."

While the blue lotus flower is demonstrably not a source of alkaloids, it has proved to be a good source of flavinoids. Flavinoids are the natural, health-giving colouring agents found in many fruits and vegetables; it is the flavinoids that give the lotus its blue colour. Today flavinoids are taken in concentrated form in herbal health preparations such as ginkgo biloba, a plant that has been used in Chinese medicine for thousands of years to ward off the effects of old age and, by boosting peripheral circulation, improve mental alertness and short-term memory.

Garner and Counsell compared their blue lotus results with a sample obtained from a commercial preparation of ginkgo. The two flavinoid profiles showed so many points of similarity that it seemed reasonable to suppose that the blue lotus and ginkgo biloba would have similar effects on their consumers. Dr Liz Williamson, an expert on the effect of chemicals on brain function, has listed these effects: "We are using ginkgo for a lot of different conditions but the main one is probably for age-related deteriorations. It is known as a kind of anti-ageing herb. It's a free-radical scavenger and an anti-oxidant, and has particularly been shown to be useful in mild Alzheimer and memory dysfunctions and various conditions where blood flow is at fault—migraine, tinnitus and so forth. It even has a sort of Viagra effect."

Would the ancient Egyptians have recognized the long-term health-giving effects of the blue lotus? Egypt was a young society. Although life expectancy was approximately forty-five to fifty years many failed to reach middle age: the hazards associated with pregnancy, childbirth and infancy plus the dangers of workplace accidents took a heavy toll on the population. Although there were indeed some elderly Egyptians, with Asru herself probably living over sixty years, it seems unlikely that the mental deteriorations of old age that trouble our own society were ever a serious problem. However, some of the more immediate effects of the blue lotus—in particular its supposed "herbal Viagra" effect—may well have been recognized and appreciated. Unfortunately, the scarcity of blue lotus plants makes it difficult to conduct a scientifically controlled experiment to monitor these effects.

Ever since the first western explorers published the vibrant images seen on the tomb walls, the whole world has known that the dynastic Egyptians loved a good, drunken party:

> That the Egyptian women were not forbidden the use of wine, nor the enjoyment of other luxuries, is evident from the frescoes which represent their feasts; and the painters, in illustrating this fact, have sometimes sacrificed their gallantry to a love of caricature. Some call the servants to support them as they sit, others with difficulty prevent themselves from falling on those behind them; a basin is brought too late by a reluctant servant and the faded flower, which is ready to drop from their heated hands, is intended to be characteristic of their own sensations.
>
> Sir J. Gardiner Wilkinson,
> *The Ancient Egyptians:Their Life and Customs* (1854)

If the Egyptians were using the blue lotus to enhance their sex lives, either in this existence or in the next, can we assume that the lotus was included in these scenes as a symbol of sexual potency, perhaps the potency necessary to rejuvenate the deceased? All Egyptologists would agree that the primary purpose of Egyptian tombs was not to store the dead body, but to assist the deceased to achieve eternal life. We might therefore expect to find that the scenes on the walls are not provided as decoration, but to somehow assist the deceased. The extent to which these walls can be decoded by modern observers is a matter of opinion. To some, including Sir J. Gardiner Wilkinson, they merely represent a vision of the ideal life beyond death.

Lise Manniche goes further in her analysis, identifying many coded references. The banqueting scenes become scenes of rejuvenation incorporating the lotus which has become a symbol of sexuality: "It is not just a picture of a good party in ancient Egypt. They wear lotus garlands round their necks; some of them have lotus flowers decorating their hair; they hold lotus flowers in their hands. The lotus flower is all over the place and it is a very large lotus flower; it is larger than life."

The Egyptian language was composed of both consonants and vowels. However, it was written using only the consonants, with the vowels entirely omitted. The ancient reader, understanding the context, would be able to insert the vowels and read words with little or no confusion. The modern reader has more of a problem; by convention "e" is inserted in the place of the missing vowels. The fact that many Egyptian words looked similar but were presumably pronounced differently allowed great scope for jokes. Manniche believes that the tomb artists deliberately included visual puns, or plays on words, which would have been obvious to their original audience but which are less so today. The many images of nubile serving girls pouring wine for the guests provide a good example of her reasoning. The word "pour," *sti*, or *seti*, looked like the word "ejaculate" (and, indeed like the word "shoot"), suggesting that both drinking and shooting scenes may have carried a hidden message of sexual potency and rebirth. This may explain why there are so many tomb scenes involving the pouring of drinks but few that actually show eating.

The Egyptians were not always averse to depicting the sexual act. However, explicit scenes of intercourse would have been considered out of place in a temple or a tomb, where tradition dictated that a more restrained canon of images had to be used. The Turin Papyrus, recovered from Deir el-Medina, is at the opposite end of the pornographic spectrum. Here, in a curious juxtapositioning, amusing animal illustrations lie alongside erotic scenes which, although now badly damaged, leave very little to the imagination. Several attractive young ladies—prostitutes?—employ a variety of sexual positions to excite a motley band of men—clients?—equipped with unfeasibly large phalluses. The purpose of this papyrus is not obvious and various unconfirmed theories have been put forward: is it simple smut? Does it illustrate the adventures of a temple priest? Or are we looking at the earliest known sex manual?

Two examples suffice to demonstrate the nature of the Turin illustrations. In one instance we see a woman sitting in a provocative manner on a chair with her legs in the air. In front of her stands a man with an erect penis. The woman talks to the man: "Contain your pleasure; your penis is within me . . . ." Another scene shows a woman sitting with her legs apart on an upturned jar with a pointed base. As she paints her lips, a man watches, entranced. In both these scenes the ladies wear little apart from the large lotus blossoms balanced on their heads.

In considering the Turin Papyrus we have come a long way in our quest to understand the role of the blue lotus in ancient ritual. We know, as did the Egyptians, that the lotus was a beautiful flower with a pleasing scent and a symbolic association with creation that made it a highly suitable offering to the gods. Thanks to modern analytical techniques we also know that chemicals within the lotus may have been effective in treating some of the deteriorations of old age. We may guess, but cannot prove, that the lotus was being consumed, perhaps in wine, to enhance sexual potency. Did Asru, elderly by the standards or her society and denied any effective pain relief, consume the lotus in order to stay young? We will probably never know.

CHAPTER THIRTEEN

Why?
Life
and Death
of a Chantress

> Go up into Gilead, and take balm, O virgin, the daughter of
> Egypt: in vain shalt thou use many medicines; for thou shalt
> not be cured.
>
> *Jeremiah* 46: 11

A COMBINATION OF ARCHAEOLOGICAL, WRITTEN AND MEDICAL EVIDENCE NOW
allows us to partially reconstruct the life and death of the lady Asru. In so
doing, we are able to gain an insight into hitherto hidden aspects of upper-
class dynastic society.

Asru was born during the Third Intermediate Period, at a time when
southern Egypt was ruled by the high priests of Amen based at Thebes,
and northern Egypt was ruled by the kings of Tanis. Although officially a

period of disunity, relationships between the two ruling houses were good and Egypt remained relatively stable throughout Asru's lifetime. This stability allowed the gods and the élite to maintain their traditional, comfortable lifestyles, and it allowed the undertakers to perfect their art. Asru's own top-quality mummification, and her two expensive wooden coffins, show us that she was a wealthy individual. The inscriptions on her coffins make reference to her matrilineal descent, and confirm that she worked in the Karnak temple where she served as a chantress, or singer.

The massive, stone-built Karnak temple complex dominated a city of low-lying mud-brick buildings. Here, in the most magnificent temple of all, lived Amen, the Hidden One, a golden statue housed in the gloom of the innermost sanctuary. Nearby were the temples where dwelt his wife, Mut, and his son, Khonsu. Egyptian temples cannot be equated with western cathedrals, synagogues or mosques. The temple was in a very literal sense the home of the resident god or goddess, and as such was forbidden to the general public who had no official part to play in the worship of the state pantheon. Access to the gods was at all times strictly controlled; even when the god himself decided to leave his sanctuary and process through the streets, he remained hidden behind the curtains of his portable shrine. Only the foremost parts of the temple, decorated with scenes of royal propaganda, might occasionally be opened to admit the citizens of Thebes. Few were able to venture beyond this first courtyard. For those who did, the passage from the hot, bright, secular world to the cool, dark, perfumed interior was a mysterious journey from chaos towards total divine control. The temple itself represented the primeval mound of creation, and the floor rose and the ceiling dropped to create a feeling of increasing confinement as the priests passed along the route to the sanctuary.

Amen was an important landowner and a major employer. Outside the temple precincts, thousands toiled on his estates and in his mines. The fruit of their labours, first offered to the gods, would be used to feed and finance the temple staff, with any surpluses being stored in large warehouses within the temple grounds. At Karnak, Amen was served by an all-male priesthood supported by a full administrative staff including a professional band of male musicians of relatively low status. However, also included on the temple roll were a number of female musicians. These women were far removed from the scantily dressed musicians and dancers whom we have seen entertaining at private banquets. The temple's female musicians were all ladies of the highest rank: the wives and daughters of priests, government officials and élite workmen. As in our own society, it seems that religion was considered a suitable occupation for upper-class women who, for reasons of social propriety, were not able to take paid employment outside the home.

The precise duties of these female temple musicians are not clear, but we may guess from New Kingdom illustrations within the Karnak complex that they were required to chant or sing, to shake the sistrum (the religious rattle dedicated to the goddess Hathor), and to carry *menit* beads (a multiple strand of beads attached to a heavy counterpoise). Asru's well-preserved feet and hands suggest that she was required neither to play a stringed instrument nor to dance in the service of her god. We have no idea whether she was paid for her services, or whether she was a volunteer, but it seems likely that she received a minor share of the offerings made to the god.

Asru led a long and privileged life. We may guess that her wealth allowed her to enjoy the best of Egypt's food, drink and medicine while avoiding the manual work and overcrowded living conditions that blighted the lives of so many. She even managed to avoid or survive the perils of pregnancy and childbirth that killed many of her fellow women. Nevertheless, Asru was ill-protected against the health hazards of her natural environment.

It has long been obvious that no Egyptian could hope to avoid toothache, the scourge of Egyptian old age caused by the inclusion of sand and grit within the food. Sand in the lungs, too, was a constant threat to those who lived in a desert environment. Now it is becoming increasingly apparent that schistosomiasis, or bilharzia infestation, was an almost inevitable result of contact with stagnant water. The River Nile brought life to Egypt, but she also brought suffering and death. Indeed, modern scientific mummy studies are starting to suggest that bilharzia was a major, invisible, killer throughout the dynastic age. Few could avoid contact with water and Egypt's doctors, unaware of the existence of the microscopic parasite, could do little to help their suffering patients.

Herodotus has his own view:

> With regard to the Egyptians themselves . . . the following mode
> of life is habitual to them. For three consecutive days each
> month they purge the body by means of emetics. This is done
> out of a regard for their health, since they believe that every dis-
> ease to which man is liable is caused by their food. Apart from
> these precautions they are, I believe, next to the Libyans, the
> healthiest people in the world; an effect of their climate, in my
> opinion, which has no sudden changes.
>
> *Histories,* Book 2: 77

Although she must have been in considerable pain from arthritis, from an old back injury, and from her various parasites, Asru does not appear to have used opium-based drugs. It is, however, possible that she took lotus blossom, perhaps mixed in wine, to promote her own feeling of well-being and to enhance her slightly failing memory. Death provided the one sure release from pain.

This evidence of universal sickness and debility is one which is entirely absent from the preserved images of upper-class dynastic life. Tomb scenes show us an élite of boundless health and vitality; royal statues provide us with a succession of strong, healthy monarchs untroubled by such de-meaning disabilities as toothache and diarrhoea; Herodotus spreads the word of Egypt's great good health. Only a few medical papyri, a handful of prayers and the bodies of the Egyptians themselves survive to suggest that all was not as the ancient artists would have us believe. This New Kingdom prayer to Amen must have been heartfelt:

> You are Amen, the Lord of the silent . . . when I call to you in my
> distress you come to rescue me. You give breath to me in my
> wretchedness and release me from my bondage.

Further Reading

The History and Excavation of Egypt

The books listed below represent an easily accessible, basic introductory course to the ancient land of Egypt and its exploration. All provide extensive bibliographies for those requiring further, more specialized, reading.

Baines, J. and Malek, J. (1980), *Atlas of Ancient Egypt*, New York.

Donadoni, S. ed. (1997), *The Egyptians*, trans. R. Bianchi *et al.*, Chicago and London.

Gardiner, A. H. (1961), *Egypt of the Pharaohs*, Oxford.

Grimal, N. (1992), *A History of Ancient Egypt*, trans. I. Shaw, Oxford.

Harris, J. R. ed. (2nd edn, 1971), *The Legacy of Egypt*, Oxford.

James, T. G. H. (1984), *Pharaoh's People: scenes from life in imperial Egypt*, Oxford.

Kemp, B. J. (1980), *Ancient Egypt: anatomy of a civilization*, London and New York.

Romer, J. (1981), *Valley of the Kings*, London.

Spencer, A. J. (1993), *Early Egypt: The rise of civilization in the Nile Valley*, London.

Trigger, B. G. *et al.* (1983), *Ancient Egypt: a social history*, Cambridge.

Case Study 1: The Lost City of the Pyramid bBuilders

There are many published books and articles relating to pyramid studies. Those listed below focus on technology—the building of the pyramids—rather than on pyramid theory, which has become a specialized field in its own right. Again, readers requiring further references should start with the bibliographies within these books.

Arnold, D. (1991), *Building in Egypt: Pharaonic Stone Masonry*, Oxford.

Clarke, S. and Engelbach, R. (1930, reprinted 1990), *Ancient Egyptian Construction and Architecture,* New York.

Cottrell, L. (1956), *The Mountains of Pharaoh: 2,000 Years of Pyramid Exploration*, London.

David, A. R. (1986), *The Pyramid Builders of Ancient Egypt: A Modern Investigation of Pharaoh's Workforce,* London.

Edwards, I. E. S. (1961 revised), *The Pyramids of Egypt,* London.

Hodges, P. and Keable, E. B. J. (1989), *How the Pyramids Were Built,* Shaftsbury.

Lehner, M. (1997), *The Complete Pyramids,* London.

Malek, J. and Forman, W. (1986), *In the Shadow of the Pyramids: Egypt during the Old Kingdom,* London.

Petrie, W. M. F. (1883), *The Pyramids and Temples of Gizeh,* London.

Quirke, S. (1992), *Ancient Egyptian Religion,* London.

Spencer, A. J. (1982), *Death in Ancient Egypt,* London.

Strudwick, N. (1985), *The Administration of Egypt in the Old Kingdom,* London.

Case Study 2: On the Trail of Tutankhamen

The Amarna Age, and the life and death of Tutankhamen, have proved highly popular with writers and researchers. An extensive list of their publications is provided in Martin, G. T. (1991), *A Bibliography of the Amarna Age and Its Aftermath,* London. The quotations from Howard Carter, cited throughout this case study, have been taken from *The Tomb of Tutankhamen.*

Aldred, C. (1988), *Akhenaten, King of Egypt,* London.

Brier, B. (1998), *The Murder of Tutankhamen,* London.

Carter, H. (1925), *The Tomb of Tutankhamen,* London, 3 volumes; reprinted 1972 in 1 volume.

Desroches-Noblecourt, C. (1963), *Tutankhamen: life and death of a pharaoh,* London and New York.

Freyling, C. (1992), *The Face of Tutankhamun,* London.

Harris, J. E. and Weeks, K. R. (1973), *X-Raying the Pharaohs,* New York and London.

Harris, J. E. and Wente, E. F. eds (1980), *An X-ray Atlas of the Royal Mummies,* Chicago.

James, T. G. H. (1992), *Howard Carter: the path to Tutankhamun,* London.

el-Mahdy, C. (1989), *Mummies, Myths and Magic,* London.

Partridge, R. B. (1994), *Faces of Pharaohs: royal mummies and coffins from ancient Thebes,* London.

Redford, D. B. (1984), *Akhenaten: the heretic king,* Princeton.

Reeves, N. (1990), *The Complete Tutankhamun: the king, the tomb, the royal treasure,* London.

Reeves, N. and Wilkinson, R. H. (1996), *The Complete Valley of the Kings,* London.

Smith, G. E. (1912), *The Royal Mummies,* Cairo.

Tyldesley, J. A. (1998), *Nefertiti: Egypt's sun queen,* London.

Case Study 3: The Chantress and the Lotus

There is no widely accessible publication on the use of drugs in ancient Egypt. The evidence for the use of opium is instead given in a series of specialized journals; those interested should consult Merrillees, R. S. (1962), "Opium Trade in the Bronze Age Levant," *Antiquity* 36: 287–92; and the articles by Klaus Koschel and Norman G. Bisset *et al.* (1994), *Egypt and the Levant: International Journal for Egyptian Archaeology and Related Disciplines* VI.

Adams, B (1984), *Egyptian Mummies*, Princes Risborough.

Andrews, C. (1984), *Egyptian Mummies*, London.

Brier, B. (1994), *Egyptian Mummies: Unravelling the Secrets of an Ancient Art*, New York.

Cockburn, A. and E. (1980), *Mummies, Disease and Ancient Cultures*, Cambridge.

David, A. R. ed. (1979), *Manchester Museum Project: Multidisciplinary Research on Ancient Egyptian Mummified Remains*, Manchester.

David, A. R. and Tapp, E. eds (1984), *Evidence Embalmed: Modern Medicine and the Mummies of Ancient Egypt*, Manchester.

David, A. R. and Archbold, R. eds (2000), *Conversations With Mummies: New Light on the Ancient Egyptians,* London.

David, A. R. and Tapp, R. (1992), *The Mummy's Tale: The Scientific and Medical Investigation of Natsef-Amun, Priest in the Temple of Karnak*, London.

Ikram, S. and Dodson, A. (1998), *The Mummy in Ancient Egypt: Equipping the Dead for Eternity*, London.

Manniche, L. (1987), *Sexual Life in Ancient Egypt*, London.

Manniche, L. (1989), *An Ancient Egyptian Herbal*, Texas.

Pettigrew, T. J. (1834), *A History of Egyptian Mummies*, London.

Reeves, C. (1992), *Egyptian Medicine*, Princes Risborough.

Taylor, J. H. (1995), *Unwrapping a Mummy*, London.

Tyldesley, J. A. (1999), *The Mummy*, London.

Ancient and Classical Texts

Diodorus Siculus, *Bibliotheca Historica*, trans. C. H. Oldfather and C. L. Sherman (1933–67), New York.

Herodotus, *The Histories*, trans. A. de Selincourt, revised with Introduction and Notes by A. R. Burn (1983), London.

Josephus, *Complete Works*, trans. W. Whiston (1976), Grand Rapids.

Kitchen, K. A. (1999), *Poetry of Ancient Egypt*, Jonsered.

Lichtheim, M. (1973–80), *Ancient Egyptian Literature*, 3 vols, Berkeley.

Parkinson, R. B. (1991), *Voices from Ancient Egypt*, London.

Simpson, W. K. ed. (1973), *The Literature of Ancient Egypt: an anthology of stories, instructions and poetry*, New Haven and London.

The Papyrus Ebers, The Greatest Egyptian Medical Document, trans. B. Ebbell (1937), Copenhagen.

The Turin Papyrus (Der Papyrus 55001 und seine Satirisch-erotischen Zeichnungen und Inschriften), trans. J.A. Omlin (1973), Turin.

Index

government, *cont.*
  maat and chaos, 24, 29
grave robbing, 123-25
Great Pyramid complex, 35-36,
    41, 48-54, 59-61
  alignment of, 80
  attendant graves, 51-52
  Khaefre's pyramid, 52-53, 59,
    74
  Menkaure's pyramid, 52, 53-54,
    74, 79
  ramps, use of, 81-83
  Sphinx, 53, 60, 104
  stone quarrying and transport,
    74-76, 80-81
  workforce requirements, 75, 79,
    81-83
Griggs, Wilfred, 97, 110, 132-33

H
hair styles, 190-91
Harris, James, 112, 131, 144, 148
Harris, John, 118
Harrison, Robert, 143, 144, 145,
    148
Hatchepsut, 77, 102-4, 105, 109,
    110, 128, 131, 147
Hathor, 116
Hawass, Zahi, 55, 64-65, 75, 82,
    83, 86, 88
health, 66-68. *See also* diseases
Herakleopolitans, 26
Herodotus, 20, 35-36, 41, 47, 50,
    52, 56-57, 62, 72, 73, 82, 85,
    163, 165-67, 191, 201-2

Hetepheres, 50-51
hieroglyphics, 10
Horemheb, 29, 145, 154,
    155-56
Horemkenesi, 173
Horus of Hierakonopolis, 40
Huni, 41
Hussein, Fawzia, 65-66
Hyksos, 26-27, 28, 98, 129

I
Illahun, 58-59
Imhotep, 39-40, 43, 46
incest, 115-17
Isis, 40, 138
Iskander, Nasry, 132
Itj-Tawy, 26

J
Josephus, 36

K
Kadesh, Battle of, 23
Kamal, Moamina, 66, 85, 86
Kamose, 98
Karnak, 22, 23, 28, 73, 100,
    101, 102, 104, 122, 153,
    200-201
Kashta, 30
Kemp, Barry, 101
Kerma, 26
Khaba, 41, 45
Khaefre, 41, 52-53, 74
Khnumnakht, 175-76
Khonsu, 200

University of Cairo, 142, 143

V

Valley of the Kings, 58, 94, 95,
    121, 122, 123-29, 133-36,
    154-55
  Ayrton's discovery, 133-36, 145
  Brugsch's discovery, 125-26
  mortuary temples replacing
      pyramid, 101-2
  Tutankhamen's tomb. *See* Tu-
      tankhamen
  workers at, 124

W

Wade, Ronald, 167
Wah, 170
Westcar Papyrus, 41

Wilkinson, Caroline, 180
Wilkinson, J. Gardiner, 196, 197
Wilkinson, Toby, 39, 53
Williamson, Liz, 195
Wilson, E., 126
women
  Akhenaten, in time of, 113-19
  Asru, study of. *See* Asru
  pyramid workers, 87-88
  queens in New Kingdom, 98,
      102-4
Woodward, Scott, 95, 115-16,
    132-33
Wurzburg University Museum,
    190

Z

Zawiyet el-Aryan, 45

About the Author

JOYCE TYLDESLEY holds a doctorate from Oxford University and is an Honorary Research Fellow at the School of Archaeology, Classics, and Oriental Studies at Liverpool University. She is the author of numerous works on Ancient Egypt, including *Nefertiti: Egypt's Sun Queen, Hatchepsut: The Female Pharaoh,* and *Daughters of Isis.*